"Do you ever ask yourself why there is so little class analysis applied to the assimilation of the 'gay movement,' or even of the previously glamorous and revolutionary 'subcultures' denoted by the word 'queer,' why today's 'activists' are so keen on reformist political strategies, why the current LGBTQQIP2SAA configuration used to describe the 'gay' or 'queer' community indicates a factionalization of sexual identity that has become so inclusive as to become almost meaningless? I have, and if you have too, Gilles Dauvé's *Your Place or Mine? A 21st Century Essay on (Same) Sex* is the right book to be holding in your hands."
—Bruce LaBruce

Your Place or Mine?
A 21st Century Essay
On (Same) Sex

Gilles Dauvé

Your Place or Mine? A 21st Century Essay On (Same) Sex
© Gilles Dauvé
This edition © 2022 PM Press.

ISBN: 978–1–62963–945–1 (paperback)
ISBN: 978–1–62963–958–1 (ebook)
Library of Congress Control Number: 2021945133

Cover art by Marc Lepson
Interior design by briandesign

10 9 8 7 6 5 4 3 2 1

PM Press
PO Box 23912
Oakland, CA 94623
www.pmpress.org

Printed in the USA

Contents

"Nowhere does one meet such density, such stupidity,
as in the questions pertaining to love and sex."
Emma Goldman, 1906

"He'd rather the man be a pervert than a policeman."
Patricia Highsmith, 1955

"We live in a sex-negative and ignorant world."
Pat—now Patrick—Califia, 1992

"Does this look sexual to you?"
Lee, in *Secretary*, directed by Steven Shainberg, 2002

We'wha in Washington

An Indian Princess

In 1886, a Zuni Indian stayed six months in Washington, DC, invited by anthropologist Matilda Coxe Stevenson. We'wha (1849–1896) met scientists, politicians, even President Cleveland, became a momentary celebrity, and socialites admired this Zuni's pottery and weaving skills. Photographs show a tall, strong figure clad in a long tunic with "ethnic" patterns. Everyone, including Matilda, who had lived in We'wha's New Mexico pueblo for a few years, thought their visitor was a woman, possibly an Indian princess.

In fact, We'wha was what anthropologists came to call a *berdache*, in order to identify what they perceived as feminine Native men. Indeed, they were puzzled by a person with "a different balance of masculine and feminine characteristics than usually seen in masculine men and feminine women" (*Cultural Anthropology*). Born with a male body, We'Wha wore women's clothes and engaged in activities normally reserved for women. Such a person was sometimes looked down upon, sometimes revered, played a special part in various ceremonies and rites, was supposed to have healing powers, and could act as a matchmaker and a mediator in cases of "couple crises." He had sexual relations with men and could become a man's second wife. Crazy Horse was said to have one or two *twinktes* (the Sioux word for *berdache*). When he died, We'wha was buried in a mixture of men's and women's clothing.

This category is believed to have existed in over a hundred Indian tribes. There were also woman "berdaches" in about thirty tribes, born with a female body and acting like men. In fact, whether male- or female-bodied, they manifested a lot more than a reversed sexual division of labor, and clothes were far from a defining point (not all the people Europeans called "berdaches" wore women's clothes). Their social position often derived from an ability to combine traditional male and female skills. A famous Navajo man was both a trusted medicine man and a master in women's arts, and he invented a new style of weaving. A Crow woman led men into battle and had three wives. In his tribe, We'wha was an authority on Zuni religion. Sexually, "berdaches" might have relationships with people of either sex: many were not homosexual and many Native American homosexuals were not "berdaches." They probably had more kinds of sexual practices than we know of (or would understand).

Anthropology was inevitably associated with European colonialism and domination over the peoples it conquered. "Berdache" was long a blanket term applied by anthropologists to all sex/gender "deviant" roles among the Native peoples of North America, as if they all partook of a single monolithic pan-Indian culture. Actually, there were dozens, perhaps hundreds of variants, with a diversity of names. Besides, "berdache" has a strong "passive" pejorative sexual connotation, which also called for its rejection. Since the 1990s, activists, scholars, and quite a few indigenous North Americans have used the general term "Two-Spirit" (also written "two spirit" or "twospirit"), which insists on the dual spirituality embodied by these persons.

"Berdache" to Gay?

The inability of Washington's high society to identify We'wha's "sex" in 1886 had, of course, a lot to do with racism and sheer ignorance. But it also reflected the heavy weight of sexed stereotyping: a human being who behaves as a woman is supposed to behave *cannot be anything but* a woman. It took a while before Matilda Coxe Stevenson realized the truth. "There is a side to the lives of these men which must remain untold," she said.

Such confusion would be unthinkable today.

Most people might speak of "homosexuality," using a word and concept that did not exist when We'wha was born and were barely used when he died. Zuni society did not know such a thing as "homosexuality": the "berdache's" sexual preference for men (instead of women) was no decisive social marker, and "berdaches'" husbands did not form a special category.

As for today's most enlightened, they would welcome We'wha as further living proof of the fallacy of binary "sexing" and sexist thinking. What was a curious piece of folklore in 1886 (for white people) is now regarded as an example among many of the impossibility of classifying human behavior according to the man/woman, masculine/feminine dichotomy.

Just as the image of the "noble savage" was used by critics of modern mercantile civilization, so the "berdache" figure is interpreted by gender studies as an implicit forerunner of a critique of gender.

In the 1950s, "homophile" activists like Harry Hay, and, after 1970, gay Native Americans, looked for inspiration and legitimacy in the historical roots provided by the "berdache." They were using him (or her) as a sort of cultural ancestor, which he (or she) was not; none of them were "homosexuals" as we now know them. The "berdache" was neither an anomaly nor a disturbing marginal figure, even less a predecessor of today's queer. His category coexisted with other categories and respected sex hierarchy. Far from being an abnormality, the "berdache" belonged to the Zuni set of norms. If, as it seems, We'wha never corrected the Washington elite's

3

misbelief, it was because the man/woman divide was not essential to his Zuni mindset.

The Zunis' originality (and they were not unique in this respect) was to make room in the man/woman difference for a subdivision where "hybrids" could find a place, those born male but later assimilated to the female group (or vice versa for the woman "berdache"). In modern parlance, Zuni society invented its particular "inclusive" way of "integrating" young biologically male people with an inclination for what Zuni regarded as the women's world. The best proof that the "berdache" consolidated the sexual order is that, as women did, they could marry men. In their own way, they fit in with the distinction between masculinity and femininity, except here the difference was less a border than a transition zone.

This was inconceivable by the Washingtonian high society of 1886. We'wha did not raise any "gender" issue: the "social sex" concept did not exist yet, and it would have been an oddity in the US capital as much as in a pueblo.

Only in the twentieth century could the "berdache" question our modes of life and thought; we are tempted to perceive of him as borderline, on the threshold of transgression, while, in fact, he served a function within rules that differed from those of Europeans and North Americans in 1886… and today.

Neither a "homosexual" nor a "transvestite," We'wha straddled two worlds; he lived just as "homosexuality" was appearing, a long time before "gays," "queers," or "transgenders/cisgenders," before the triumph of capitalism, the first mode of production to turn "homosexuality" into a problem to be solved.

Our Goal and Method

For a long time, what is now known as homosexuality was a human practice, usually repressed or ignored, later acknowledged and theorized, yet listed as nonstandard behavior and still socially unacceptable.

How did this practice become socially visible and (to an extent and only in the supposedly "advanced" parts of the world) accepted toward the end of the twentieth century? And how did it come to define an identity? That is our (double) question.

This is neither a summary of the history of "homosexuality" nor of the theories on the subject. We will only point out successive significant historical landmarks, from the obscure origins of the category in the nineteenth century to its contemporary ascendency under an increasingly public eye in the twentieth, which has also coincided with the fragmentation of this entity: "homosexuals" are no more; there are only gays, lesbians, bisexuals, transgender persons, queers… distinct and overlapping groups, both allies and rivals, sometimes institutionalized, the aggregation of which gives an illusion of community.

If this essay often refers to the workers' movement, to socialism, to communism, to the proletarians, it is not because we wish to present a popular "counter-history" of (same)sex, but because, from Jean-Baptiste Schweitzer in 1864 to the Stonewall rioters in 1969, this has a lot to do with social history and indeed with capitalism and class struggle. Although modern society cannot be understood on the sole basis of class analysis (i.e., by the interaction between bourgeois and proletarians), we must be aware that its evolution is structured by class divisions.

"No Sex, Please, We're Marxists!"

Lack of space has forced us to edit out a lot of meaningful aspects, as well as stimulating writers like Fourier and strong statements and positions by anarchists like Erich Mühsam (1878–1934) and Emma Goldman (1869–1940). The latter was critical of those in the labor movement and on the far left who refused to address "the sex question." Over a hundred years later, a number of radicals still have a problem with the idea that class struggle involves a lot more than just class, and that an emancipatory movement can only exist as a historical force if it deals with all dimensions of human life.

As far as homosexuality is concerned, most socialists/communists ignored it, denounced it as bourgeois, or, when it occurred in jails, for example, merely used it as proof that prison degrades the human being. (We will focus on Marx and Engels in chapter 2.) This certainly was one of the differences between socialists and anarchists, though Emma Goldman regretted that some of her Italian and Jewish libertarian comrades attacked her for defending the cause of "Homo Sexuals and Lesbians." About her 1915 speaking tour in the US, she said:

> Censorship came from some of my own comrades because I was treating such "unnatural" themes as homosexuality. Anarchism was already enough misunderstood, and anarchists considered depraved; it was inadvisable to add to the misconceptions by taking up perverted sex-forms, they argued.

Their attitude, she said, came from a misunderstanding of the "intricacies of life that motivate human action": for her, accepting same-sex desire was part of the basic libertarian requirement.

A few decades later, anarchist and homosexual Daniel Guérin (1904–1988) also experienced

> homophobia in the socialist and labor movements [and] lived what he referred to as a cruel dichotomy. With friends and comrades to whom he felt quite close, and in whom he was able to confide as far as other things were concerned, Guérin nevertheless had to bite his tongue and refrain from raising anything to do with sexuality, and it was certainly inconceivable that he should ever attempt to defend a non-orthodox

version of love, even from a detached point of view.
(David Berry)

To be faithful to historical truth, this section title is a bit unfair to Marxists: it should be extended to include quite a few past (and possibly present) anarchists, syndicalists, labor activists...

CHAPTER 1

The Invention of "Sexuality"

"Sexuality has a history—though not a very long one."
—David Halperin

A New Social Object

Both the word *sexuality* and the concept appeared in the nineteenth century and early twentieth centuries, achieving public recognition in 1905 with Freud's *Three Essays on the Theory of Sexuality*. The realities delineated by this term (and others like "sadism" and "masochism," interestingly both coined after novelists) had existed for a long time, but only at that point entered political management and public discourse as a specific object because of the need to stake out a domain of human activity that was becoming "an issue."

In the eighteenth century, Diderot's *Encyclopaedia* gave a classified inventory of sciences, trades, crafts, and arts, as if, Goethe said, we were visiting "a large factory." To catalogue the whole of creation, the ascending industrial mercantile world needed to give specific names to everything, from human behavior to nature and machinery. This was the first society in which everyone was primarily defined by his place in the productive system. The bourgeoisie systematized knowledge and technique to enhance firms' productivity, not just the wealth of a sovereign or a country. Parallel to economic science, assisted by sociology and psychology, a political economy of population was born, with demography as a particular field of knowledge. A system typified by productivity and standardization cannot do without defining norms.

The seventeenth and eighteenth centuries saw an abundance of manuals rich in details about sexual organs and intercourse, providing educators and mothers with moral and practical advice, even insisting on the clitoris as a focus of pleasure. But these books linked sexual activity with human reproduction; when they suggested how to achieve fulfilling coition, the purpose was to ensure the well-being of a stable family couple and successful procreation contributing to the social order. In contrast, "sexuality" later came on stage when sexual relations were thought of as possibly having another purpose beyond propagating the species, and they ceased to be regarded as merely "natural." Unlike the traditional rural way of life, the industrial metropolis fostered celibacy, unmarried coupling, casual sex, and prostitution, which made sexual activity distinct from procreation increasingly visible. A society centered on production (of capital, of profit, of humans), particularly by locking woman into a productive role at home and in the workshop, had to understand and manage whatever *does not fit in* with production and, therefore, in sexual relations, whatever does not partake of reproduction.

The new social object called "sexuality" was necessary to encompass elements different from (and sometimes in conflict with) patriarchy, procreation, child care, education, heritage transmission, etc. It was composed out of parts borrowed from other mental frameworks: natural science, medicine, eroticism, etc. Family and sexuality overlap but do not coincide.

Later, with common access to contraception, the decoupling of sexual acts from reproduction was to go much further, but the evolution had started at least one century earlier. For this distinct sphere to exist, it needed the advent of wage labor, which set the productive time-space apart from the rest of social activities to an extent previously unimaginable. If everything has to be productive, not only does the value production moment in the factory have to be specified but also that which reproduces proletarians in the family—hence, an unprecedented sexual regulation.

There had been populations before, of course, and population administration: Luke says that Jesus was born in Bethlehem because his parents had to travel to their place of origin for a Roman census. But capitalism is the first mode of production to set up systematic institutions in order to facilitate the best possible reproduction of labor power via health care bodies, public (preventive medicine, municipal health centers, etc.) as well as private (bourgeois-financed and run). For famous alienist Jean-Étienne Dominique Esquirol, mental disease was "a disease of civilization." (*Maladies mentales*, 1838) Later, in *The Nationalisation of Health* (1892), social reformer and sex studies explorer Havelock Ellis asserted that the state should be responsible for the health of its citizens. A nineteenth century committed to productive models could not fail to investigate whatever crossed the line; it had to interpret and manage whatever it set aside. As before, ethics and science walked hand in hand to define sexual concourse in relation to healthy procreation; the difference was that now they also had to take in account what stood outside the realm of "normality." Setting the rule implied acknowledging, understanding, and impeding conduct that broke the rule.

Non-procreative sexuality as the flip side of the norm included prostitution, stigmatized yet accepted as the inevitable evil counterpart. Family reproduction with the wife, sex and pleasure with the prostitute, providing Dr. Jekyll could control Mr. Hyde. Law, science, and ideology illustrated the attraction/repulsion fed by this duality. Fin de siècle art is replete with images of masculine fiascos, of androgynous creatures, of misogynist decadents and threatening femmes fatales. Bram Stoker's *Dracula* (1897) expresses the fear of and fascination with nonreproductive sex: the vampire knows neither birth nor death.

Dissolution of Bonds

As is well known, the nineteenth-century bourgeois harnessed religious morals, family values, and submissive habits to enforce discipline in the mines and textile mills. Yet, at the same time, wage labor meant husband, wife, and children were working outside the home, thereby undermining the family as the basic economic unit for craft and trade. Meanwhile, in the case of the bourgeoisie, family ownership was being eroded by the progress of the joint-stock company.

> The dissolute bourgeois evades marriage and secretly commits adultery; the merchant evades the institution of property by depriving others of property by speculation, bankruptcy, etc.; the young bourgeois makes himself independent of his own family, if he can in fact abolish the family as far as he is concerned. But marriage, property, the family ... are the practical basis on which the bourgeoisie has erected its domination, and because in their bourgeois form they are the conditions which make the bourgeois a bourgeois....
> So the family remains because it is made necessary by its connection with the mode of production, which exists independently of the will of bourgeois society. (Karl Marx and Frederick Engels, *German Ideology*, 1846)

The question is: What family?

Marx's contemporaries observed a dissolution of traditional ties. Some bemoaned the loss; others rejoiced over the coming of a beneficial "universalism." Quoting Saint Paul—"There is neither Jew nor Gentile, neither slave nor free, nor is there male and female, for you are all one in Christ Jesus," Galatians, 3:28—Hegel heralded the dawn of an era when man would no longer be valued as Greek, Roman, or Jew or depend upon his birth status: he would have "an infinite value in himself as man." Wage labor would potentially liberate the individual from the bonds of blood, origin, nature, soil... *and biological sex*.

As the capitalist mode of production tends to treat all human beings as productive factors, it benefits from the inequality of the sexes; yet it also must promote labor market fluidity and the interchangeability of individuals—be they man or woman, Christian or Muslim, white or a person of color, believer or atheist... *hetero or homo*.

The Sexologist and the Doodlebug

The ascending bourgeoisie negated neither sex nor the body; it organized them. Regulation increasingly took on the form of banning.

The words *sexuality* and *sexualism* go back to the nineteenth century, based on the much older *sex*, which most etymologists agree comes from the Latin *sexus, to divide or cut*, meaning that humans (at least a vast majority of them) are biologically either male or female. That is a partition— *and* conjunction—constitutive of human existence. The verb *to sex* appeared at the end of the nineteenth century, meaning *to determine the sex of* (as in a "chicken sexer"): "sexing" marks out a fundamental difference, a supposedly unbridgeable gap.

A definition separates one meaning from the neighboring meanings, so the classifier's skill lies in his ability to reconnect what he has disconnected. A difficult task for dictionary editors but a strenuous exertion for sex analyzers. Medical science was busy correlating acts and biological data in a hundred different ways according to the chosen criterion, multiplying typologies and neologisms. Cutting up requires adequate glue. Krafft-Ebing, best-selling author of *Psychopathia Sexualis*, "with its special reference to Contrary

Sexual Instinct" (the 1884 edition was followed by many others), and a leading authority on the subject popularized a string of wordings, one of which had to wait about a hundred years before enjoying widespread currency: *pedophilia*. The success of an expert or a school of thought can be measured first by the diffusion of its neologisms from the scientific community to the educated public, then into everyday speech—*pedophile* being currently shortened to *pedo*.

Science faced a major conundrum: Was man-man attraction to be explained as inborn, as degeneration, as a moral failure, as a personal/psychological crisis, or possibly as having sociological causes?

This puzzle launched a lengthy divisive debate among psychiatrists, as well as biologists and entomologists, to determine whether human "perversions" also occur in the animal kingdom: "pervert" signifying what does not directly benefit reproductive sex, as Richard von Krafft-Ebing made quite clear. In the second half of the nineteenth century, an amazing array of experiments were conducted to research onanism and male-male sex with rats, doodlebugs (*melolontha vulgaris*), and silkworm mulberries: Was their "pederasty" driven "by opportunity" or "by taste"? Was it "accidental or acquired"? If animals are familiar with same-sex relations, then it pertains to nature. On the contrary, if it derives from particular circumstances, for example, life in a confined environment (for men: boarding schools, barracks, prisons, etc.), it comes within the alienists' remit to deal with it.

Bizarre as it may appear to the modern eye (it is always easy to make fun of yesterday's most blatant scientific misconceptions), there was no aberration in a debate that involved a power struggle. When the "nurture" thesis prevailed over the "nature" thesis, to use twentieth-century vocabulary, it gave preeminence to doctors and (re)educators. Contemporary science almost unanimously declared same-sex relations to be a deviation from "normal" attraction between the two sexes, effectively going the wrong way, which accounts for the long lifespan of the word *invert*. The homosexual's pathology was to suffer from a contradiction between his anatomy and his desire, and psychiatry's job was to reconcile the two. As a result, medicine and justice would join forces, doctors regularly being called into court as expert witnesses.

Civilized Morals and Nervous Illness

Contrary to common misbelief, sexual desire and activity are not incompatible with productive labor: "sexuality" was created as a category to help make it productive (of children, but of more than that). The capitalist mode of production is not hostile to pleasure, as long as pleasure proves profitable.

In the nineteenth-century, people gradually came to live with the idea that same-sex love was not a sin, simply a disease, like tuberculosis, albeit possibly a criminal one, which TB was not. Though it was no longer perceived of as blasphemous and devilish, as a violation of God's command, it still disrupted man's law, threatened public order, and called for diffuse and indirect control, which implied naming and classifying and, indeed, involved a lot more than social medicine. Let's just mention the "invention" of *sport*, for example, this truly modern phenomenon, a concentrate of capitalist fundamentals, which manages at the same time to discipline the body, to measure efforts and achievements, to benchmark competing individuals, and to promote team spirit, while developing hero worship and, let's not forget, nationalist passion.

Though it claims to be accountable to nothing but itself, psychoanalysis fit into this set-up. Sigmund Freud's continuing prominence for over a century has less to do with the intrinsic value of his most famous concepts (the Oedipus complex, particularly) than with his ability to systematize a permanent state of crisis, summed up in his 1908 text, tellingly titled *Civilized Sexual Morality and Modern Nervous*

Illness. Until then, moralists invoked supposedly unalterable principles. Freud's novelty was to assume that the individual, instead of trying to obey eternal moral standards, could find his own way to psychological balance—under proper psychiatric guidance, of course. The family had previously been a model but was now regarded as a nexus of contradictions to untangle. Childhood had once been a learning phase, when the elders taught you what to do, but was now a moment of risk, when your mother and father could equally do you good or hurt you—probably both. Previously, one had to respect traditions; now one was asked to do whatever would make him or her part of society with as little harm done as possible. Sexual morality became secular, requiring a shift from Law to laws.

The moment the paterfamilias started to be questioned was also the point at which he became a theoretical object. The central father figure was no longer taken for granted, and the bourgeois family pattern came to be seen as just as much a problem as a solution, and more pathogenic than healthy. The Freudian system provided "Western civilization" with a means to interpret the crisis of the family and the transformation of the relations between sexes. "Id, ego, superego," what a comforting threesome... surrealist (and gay) René Crevel said Freud had done away with the "normal man" only to reduce human complexity to an "abstract mannequin," and Karl Kraus aptly described psychoanalysis as that mental illness that regards itself as therapy.

Concerning same-sex love, Freud thought that in early childhood everyone is bisexual and evolves to be attracted to the other sex, except the homosexual who (usually after a distressing experience) interrupts what should have been normal development. Everybody develops through stages; unfortunately, the homosexual stops part way. If Freud believed it was barely possible to "cure" a homosexual, that was because he took seriously (a lot more so than most of his colleagues, disciples, and successors) the fundamental bisexuality and sexual *polymorphism* of human beings. Freud, ever the conservative pessimist, did not regard homosex as any more equivocal and opaque than heterosex, because for him medicine at best alleviates the misery of a life that never fully escapes anxiety and suffering.

This required a thorough cataloguing of disorderliness. "Please, let's put a little order in these orgies, some is necessary even in the bosom of delirium and infamy," Sade wrote in 1795. With the same obsession for classification and a lot less imagination, psychiatrists have kept putting disorder in order, itemizing and indexing perversions as if they were dealing with varieties of outlandish biological species. They even received help from amateur scientists with a taste for compiling and filing. Thomas N. Painter (1905–1978), a gay activist-researcher, who gathered 11,000 pages (with 2,700 pictures) of sexual records, met Alfred Kinsey and became his unpaid assistant for a while (more on Kinsey in chapter 4).

Documenting anomalies did not prevent some measure of tolerance: Krafft-Ebing and Freud were not alone in the medical profession in opposing the criminalization of homosexuality. Mapping what crosses the line into the abnormal helped psychologists and doctors become specialists in behavioral peacemaking and reconditioning. When capitalist society relied less on prohibition than on the norm, it had to be aware of misbehavior in order to correct it. Sex was not silenced—it was given articulated speech. Later, in the twilight of the twentieth century, as capitalist domination went deeper, normalizing social mores was to become compatible with a wide range of norms.

Class Analysis vs. Discourse Analysis, or the Flaw in Foucault

The bourgeois cared less about (im)proper morality than about his material interests. Labor had to be submitted, subordinated to the dictates of the foreman and the machine, and trained to conform to workshop discipline and time constraints. Public health policies administered to the laboring masses gradually took over habitat, urban planning, hygiene, child reproduction, education, and immigration. Everything had to be recorded, quantified, and measured, from skull dimension assessments to time-and-motion studies—even to an absurd point, such as the nineteenth-century obsession with masturbation, denounced as a waste of energy.

For example, while prostitution had often been an officially organized trade (as in municipal medieval brothels) or a repressed profession (prostitutes being locked up or deported), it was now dealt with by heath care policy, regulated, and in some countries registered and medically inspected.

That being said, social spending remained a very small proportion of state budgets until 1914. Its evolution was quite slow and only developed under the combined pressures of proletarian struggles, the rise of the workers' movement, and political and military imperatives. Population administration was determined by social causes that were first and foremost class relations.

Throughout the nineteenth century, the bourgeois kept denouncing the immoral and unhygienic life of the "Great Unwashed," the uneducated, uncouth worker, a near savage on the edge of vagrancy, madness, and crime. Doctors and sociologists (sociology as a science being another nineteenth-century creation) expertly demonstrated that incest was to be found mostly in the laboring classes, where bodily proximity led to promiscuousness and a return to quasi animal life. Until the mid-twentieth century, university pundits would describe the workers as degenerate. Those who could be a threat to social order were classified as inferior and deviant.

This sequence of causes is precisely what Foucault disregarded, preferring to reduce capitalism to the institution of disciplinarian and biopolitical power technologies, of which the capital/labor relation is a mere consequence. The wealth of material written for or by middle- and upper-class women was enough for Foucault to conclude that monitoring bourgeois sexuality had preeminence over organizing proletarian reproduction. He pulled a single thread and spun it into the whole story.

Historically, the determinant is the dependence of the proletarians—women and men—on earning cash for a livelihood, their subordination to productive labor to earn it, and all that goes with that to ensure the reproduction of the system.

Foucault turned this historical causation upside-down. For him, capitalist society does not produce value accumulated by labor; it produces control and direct or oblique subjugation. In his view, what matters is the institutions that codify and reproduce forms of power, and he explained history as the movement from one type of power to another. Critical theory is reduced to a genealogy of domination processes, where the capital/labor relation is but one control structure among many. Moreover, giving the first volume of his *History of Sexuality* the title *The Will to Knowledge* (1976) took Foucault one step further; as he trawled through a vast archive of memory artefacts, he equated power techniques with power discourses, as if society were ruled by what it says and believes about itself.

It is significant that in the last decades the word *discourse* has by and large replaced *ideology*. However pompous and formulaic "ideology" often was (targeting "bourgeois ideology" at every turn), at least it tried to remain connected to some elemental social realities, whereas "discourse" can and indeed must pertain to just about anything. Logically, if language is power and vice versa, then society is shaped by language, so change the words and you will change the world. First, class was swapped for domination. Second, domination forms were toned down to communication forms and action downsized to expression. In that respect, Foucault's legacy has some bearing on (homo)sexual matters, namely the "war of words" examined in chapter 8, as well as on "postmodern" thinking, as we will see in chapter 11 on "queer."

The American Plan, or "Progressive" US Biopolitics

History helps clarify the social causes of biopolitics, as shown in the US.

The United States' Progressive Era, from the 1890s to the 1920s, is mainly remembered for its "citizens' democracy," philanthropy, political reform (extension of women's suffrage), economic reform (anti-trust laws to promote "fair competition" and the creation of the Federal Reserve), moralization of public life (anti-corruption campaigns) and of private life (Prohibition).

More to the point, progressives thought science and technology could cure social ills by providing increased control over the common people—especially the poor. Morality also applied abroad and legitimized the imperialist role of the US as the rightful police force, which sent troops to the Caribbean, occupied the Philippines, intervened in Europe in 1917, etc.

If we limit ourselves to our subject, the Progressive Age implemented a biopolitical *law and order* policy in the name of public welfare. Its social hygiene movement justified "moral purges, intimate surveillance of women's reproductive choices, separation of children from parents, and the indefinite detention of those deemed 'unfit.'" (Patricia J. Williams: all subsequent related quotes are hers) The aim was to contain the conflated issues of "delinquency," "immorality," "feeblemindedness," and "imbecility," sorting out the deserving from the undeserving poor: "Pauperism became a social disease." Backed by typologies and statistics, a public health plan, known as the American Plan, was meant to curb the spread of sexually transmitted diseases, not by regulating prostitution (as in France, for example) but by treating it as a near-criminal act. Under the guise of preventing venereal disease was a nationwide effort to discourage extramarital sex, to clean up the streets, and to police women's behavior.

Needless to say, this was openly racist, with an emphasis on Nordic purity and a rejection of "miscegenation." Sterilizing "unfit" human stock went with restrictions on immigration from Eastern and Southern Europe and the "Americanization" of recent immigrants via education. Most women affected by the American Plan were women of color.

Many US states passed ordinances "limiting the ability of people deemed unpleasant-looking to move about in public without licences." Physical appearance was turned into a social standard. Surgical sterilization was imposed on grounds that fused medical and class motives, with the notion of "social disease" combining poverty, idleness, and waywardness. Child welfare and criminal justice both emerged and merged in the twentieth century, and interracial sex and prostitution were a priority target. In the particular circumstances of the United States, "sexuality" was becoming a concept, a political object, and an indispensable aspect of public policy.

One last example, perhaps the most emblematic biopolitical experiment: the post-1945 Welfare State in Britain. In his famous 1942 report that was to launch that program, William Beveridge argued that because of the fall of the birth rate in the UK in the 1930s, "with its present reproduction rate, the British race cannot continue." The plan extended wartime mobilizing and managing of the labor force by means adapted to a peace economy. The five "Giant" enemies targeted by Beveridge were Want, Disease, Ignorance, and Squalor, as well as *Idleness*, and the Welfare State aimed at "a system to include everyone [the sick, the old, women at home, and children], while keeping the incentive to work." (Andrew Marr)

CHAPTER 2

The Invention of "Homosexuality"

This is no linear history, and now is the time for a little detour.

"Male-Female" vs. "All-Female" Political Lines

In the 1860s, one of the leading German socialist figures, now long forgotten by history, was accused of being a boy-lover and the story was later "raked again and again by his political opponents" (Hubert Kennedy)—Marx and Engels included.

In 1863, the first workers' organization of national importance in Germany was born: the General German Workers' Association (ADAV, by its German acronym), led by Ferdinand Lassalle. It advocated associated labor, "in which the working class becomes its own employer," but sought Bismarck's support against the bourgeoisie, as if state-backed cooperatives could build "socialism from above." While he regarded the ADAV as a positive step forward, Marx was critical of Lassalle's "statism" and wished for autonomous working-class action.

In 1862, one of the pioneers of social democracy in the Frankfurt region, Johann Baptist Schweitzer (1833–1875), was accused by two witnesses, with little "hard evidence" (Hubert Kennedy), of having incited a fourteen-year-old boy to an "indecent act" in a park. The teenager (or the young man, as his age remained uncertain) disappeared, and we know nothing more about him. Schweitzer denied the accusation, yet was condemned to two weeks in prison for violation of public decency, which resulted in him being ostracized by most friends and comrades. For example, in 1863, the Frankfurt section of the ADAV refused him membership. Schweitzer commented:

> When those in my hometown who called themselves my friends believed that the time had finally come when they could let loose their pent-up envy, when so many credulously repeated what a few had invented, I asked myself in astonishment, "How have you deserved this?" But that was only the first quick moment—and it occurred to me that it was always like that and would remain so forever.

Lassalle, however, saw in this persona non grata (who had published a political novel that could be regarded as good socialist propaganda) a promising recruit and had him accepted into the Leipzig section. "What relation is there between political practice and a sexual abnormality?" Lassalle asked. But when Schweitzer wished to speak in Frankfurt, the local leader refused: "we cannot use him as a person. He is dead here."

Lassalle replied:

> The abnormality attributed to Dr. von Schweitzer has nothing whatever to do with his political character. I need only remind you that, however incomprehensible such unnatural tastes appear to us, the tendency of which Dr. von Schweitzer is accused was the general rule among the ancient Greeks, their statesmen and their philosophers. Ancient Greece saw nothing wrong in it, and I consider the great Greek philosophers and the Greek people knew the meaning of morality.... I could understand your not wishing Dr. von Schweitzer to marry your daughter. But why not think, work, and struggle in his company? What has any department of political activity to do with sexual abnormality?

And he wrote to Schweitzer: "I will never hide the fact that I maintain for you the greatest respect and hold you in the highest regard."

After Lassalle's death in a duel in 1864, Schweitzer became head of the ADAV. He was sentenced to one year in prison for his attacks on the government, and later amnestied. In 1867, he was elected to the new parliament of the North German Confederation at the Reichstag, one of the very first self-proclaimed socialist MPs in Europe.

Marx, on the other hand, associated (with strong reservations) with the socialists led by August Bebel and Wilhelm Liebknecht, who founded the Social Democratic Party in 1869, in opposition to the ADAV. From then on, the "Lassallist" Schweitzer became an inevitable political partner *and rival*: in politics one weapon is as good as another; it often comes down to "who hates whom," and slander is commonplace.

On March 10, 1865, Marx wrote to Engels: "You must arrange for a few jokes about the fellow [Schweitzer] to reach Siebel [1836–1868, a friend of Marx's], for him to hawk around in the various papers." What jokes Marx had in mind is easy to guess. Since 1862, the "Frankfurt incident," embellished and exaggerated, had given rise to gossip and scandal-mongering that Schweitzer's opponents took pleasure in repeating or simply alluding to. In June 22, 1869, in a letter to Marx on a recent merger between a group supported by Sophie von Hatzfeldt, nicknamed "the Red Countess" (1805–1881), and the ADAV, Engels spoke of a "male-female line" (the one with Sophie), and the "all-female line of the Lassalleans," "female" referring to the rumors about Schweitzer's sexual orientation.

The rift widened between the Social Democratic Party and Schweitzer's followers, who kept on expecting support from the state and sided with the Prussian government in the war against France in 1870. Later, the two parties merged at the Gotha congress (1875), about which Marx wrote his

Critique of the Gotha Programme, but this is beyond the scope of our study.

By then, Schweitzer had stepped down as chair of the ADAV, and had even been excluded from the party in 1872 (on the grounds of the misappropriation of party funds). Repudiated by his former comrades, Schweitzer launched a second career as a playwright. No workers attended his funeral.

In all of this, the "sexual question" remained an aside for all protagonists, who did not see in it a social or political question. In Schweitzer's case, Lassalle was supporting one of his followers, while Marx and Engels were hardly picky in their choice of weapons against an adversary. A "private matter" for Lassalle and ammunition for petty calumny for Marx and Engels.

The concept of "homosexuality" did not yet exist, although…

"A Female Psyche in a Male Body"

On June 22, 1869, Engels wrote to Marx:

> The *Urning* you sent me is a very curious thing. These are extremely unnatural revelations. The paederasts are beginning to count themselves, and discover that they are a power in the state. Only organisation was lacking, but according to this source it apparently already exists in secret. And since they have such important men in all the old parties and even in the new ones, from Rösing to Schweitzer, they cannot fail to triumph. *Guerre aux cons, paix aux trous-du-cul* [War to the cunts, peace to the assholes] will now be the slogan…. Incidentally it is only in Germany that a fellow like this can possibly come forward, convert this smut into a theory…. If Schweitzer could be made useful for anything, it would be to wheedle out of this peculiar honourable gentleman the particulars of

the paederasts in high and top places, which would
certainly not be difficult for him as a brother in spirit.

The "Urning" phrase came from a brochure which Marx
had sent to Engels, by Karl-Heinrich Ulrichs (1825–1895),
who between 1864 and 1879 published a series of booklets
expounding the theory of the *Urninge* (Uranian or Uranist),
characterized by *"a female psyche in a male body."*

While studying law at university, Ulrichs, born in the
state of Hanover, discovered his attraction to men. One of
his friends committed suicide to escape prosecution for
sodomy and the ensuing inevitable public humiliation. When
Schweitzer was brought to court for "offence against public
decency" in 1862, Ulrichs spoke in his defense. Although his
sexual orientation was not illegal in Hanover at the time,
Ulrichs was driven from public office and afterward lived off
a small inheritance and intermittent work as a journalist and
secretary. In 1864, he anonymously published *Researches on
the Enigma of Love between Men*, only acknowledging being
the author four years later. Of all his booklets on the subject,
at least one was known to Marx and Engels.

Although sodomy was not a crime under Hanoverian
law, everything changed when Prussia annexed Hanover.
Therefore, for Ulrichs, the struggle for the right to same-sex
love coincided with the fight for democratic liberties. His
house was searched, his library confiscated, and, in 1867,
he was arrested twice and served three months in prison.
Speaking to the Congress of German Jurists in Munich in 1867
against the anti-sodomy laws in force in several German states,
he was shouted down before he could finish his speech. He
was later refused membership of a scientific Frankfurt association on the basis that he claimed to belong to a third sex,
a category not recognized in the association's constitution.

Legally, it was a lost battle. After 1871, Prussian anti-sodomy law was applied to the whole of a newly unified Germany

and § 175 criminalized "unnatural sexual acts ... between men, or between men and animals" (the law ignored female homosexuality). This paragraph was to remain in force in both East and West Germany until the 1960s.

As feminist Mary Wollstonecraft had written in the year of her death (1797), "Those bold enough to advance before the age they live in ... must learn to brave censure." In 1880, Ulrichs left Germany for Italy, where he died fifteen years later in L'Aquila.

Ulrichs was not satisfied with simply defending a cause: he wanted to ground it in science—the science of his time. First, he was interested in magnetism, then he turned to embryology. From the fact that the sexual organs remain undifferentiated at the beginning of the fetus's development, Ulrichs concluded that the organism has a double sexual potentiality, which in certain individuals can produce a female spirit or soul (*anima*) in a male body. A man attracted to men is a kind of psychological hermaphrodite, whom he named *Urning*, and the female equivalent (the woman attracted to women) *Urningin*.

The choice of terms is significant. "We make up a third sex.... We are women in spirit," wrote Ulrichs, but he chose to avoid using "third sex," which he considered pejorative, and preferred to look for inspiration in ancient times, invoking mythology in support of natural science. Traditionally, Aphrodite is venerated in two aspects: Aphrodite *Ourania*, who represents "celestial love," and *Pandemos,* the incarnation of "earthly, physical love." Qualifying the man attracted to the same sex as "Urning," Ulrichs bestowed upon him a purity and elevation, the nobility of Classical Antiquity, in opposition to the low and vulgar images often associated with sex between men. Ulrichs reckoned that one adult German male in five hundred fell into this category.

With time, Ulrichs broadened his perspective to include a continuum of sexual orientations; some Urnings are born with a masculine inclination, others with a feminine one. As he realized that his theory of a female soul in a male body did not adequately map out the considerable variety of observable kinds of same-sex love, Ulrichs subdivided the categories, finishing up with a series of sixteen types.

Although he was hardly taken seriously, Ulrichs's booklets found their readers, one of them a luminary on the subject, Krafft-Ebing (1840–1902), with whom Ulrichs corresponded. Krafft-Ebing's bestseller *Psychopathia Sexualis* (the title says it all), a scientific and popular success, first published in 1886 and reprinted in many subsequent editions, subtitled *With Special Research on Sexual Inversion*, detailed no less than 238 "cases." The author distinguishes two categories of inversion: acquired and congenital. In the section on the second category, he quotes Ulrichs and repeatedly uses the word *Urning*.

"A Very Interesting Riddle of Nature"

Born in Hungary in 1824, German-language author, translator, bookseller, and journalist Karl-Maria Kertbeny moved in literary and political circles and led a restless life of European peregrinations and encounters. After Ludwig Kugelmann wrote to Marx saying that Kertbeny had paid him a visit and talked about everything and everyone, Marx replied on January 30, 1868, that he did not know this "literary busybody" personally, adding there seemed to be "nothing politically suspicious against him."

Though Kertbeny never openly stated it, his diary reveals a strong attraction to men. There was nothing impersonal about his research into same-sex love: "How do I, a normally sexed individual, ever stumble onto the existence of homosexualism…?" His work on the subject was also a self-inquiry into the trauma of what a biographer called his "double life."

The first recorded use of the word homosexuality (*Homosexualität*) was in the May 6, 1668, draft of a letter by

Kertbeny (most certainly to Ulrichs). *Homosexuality* added a Latin ending to a Greek root, which was also the case with *sociology*, invented in the late eighteenth century and popularized in the nineteenth. Kertbeny also wrote:

> To prove the innate nature [of homosexuality] is not at all useful, especially not quickly, what's more it cuts both ways, let it be a very interesting riddle of nature from the anthropological point of view … we wouldn't win anything by proving innateness. Rather, we should convince our opponents that exactly according to their legal notion they do not have anything to do with this inclination, let it be innate or voluntary, because the State does not have the right to intervene in what is happening between two consenting people aged over fourteen, excluding publicity, not hurting the rights of any third party.

Kertbeny was drawing from the natural sciences: "unisexual" and "bisexual" are botanical terms. Nevertheless, unlike Ulrichs, he was not seeking biological causes and regarded the innate/acquired controversy as irrelevant. Basically, he wished to conceive new positive categories against juridical and medical denigration and argued that the principle of equal human rights also applies in the sexual domain. In an anonymous 1869 booklet against § 143 of the Prussian statute (which prohibited "unnatural acts between men"), Kertbeny used both the words *homosexuality* and *heterosexuality*; in order to defend those accused (of sodomy, in fact), he posited two opposite and parallel sexual practices.

An object is defined by its conceptual separation from others. Kertbeny hoped to win recognition of the right to what he called homosexuality by distinguishing it from what he called heterosexuality, the category of "heterosexuality" owing its "invention" to the defenders of its opposite, a socially prohibited activity.

At the time, people spoke of a "love with no name"; both the practice *and the word* were still proscribed. The pioneers of sexual emancipation wanted to give this practice a proper name and, thereby, legitimacy: better to name oneself than to be named in a discriminatory way.

Self-Assertion by Naturalization

Against Kertbeny's advice, in the following decades most defenders of same-sex love had espoused the "innateness" thesis (which has prevailed up to our time). This option gave homosexuality a natural justification against those who denounced it as monstrous and "against nature." Ulrichs wrote about the Uranian in 1870: "His sexual orientation is a right established by Nature. Legislators have no right to veto nature." Supposing homosexuality is a biological fact, then some people are subject to an inborn attraction to the same sex, the origins of which are congenital, and, therefore, there can be no rational basis for prohibiting conducts resulting from it. If a man is not drawn to other men by choice, how could he be held responsible and sanctioned?

However, by defining a sexual practice as a new *natural* object called *homosexuality*, its defenders played into the hands of their critics. Against moral and legal condemnation of a so-called "unnatural" practice, they argued for an intrinsic specificity. This posed homosexual and heterosexual individuals as radical opposites, and even though the divergence was now given a rational basis, this difference was emphasized, which in a normalizing society entailed being segregated as "deviant."

If the homosexual is fundamentally different (granted, *in spite of himself*) because of his different physical and mental constitution, then it is not absurd for a society bent on maintaining order to try to bring him back into the fold. He is no longer a criminal, simply a patient to be treated for his own and for the social good. Psychiatry took over where the police left off. Kertbeny's formalizing of two opposite realities maintained the "problem" he intended to solve.

"Homophobic" Marx and Engels

The two most famous founding fathers of communist theory were contemporary with the early defenders of same-sex love and the inventor of the *homosexuality*, both the word and the concept, was not unknown to them. Yet Marx and Engels oscillated between indifference and aversion and reacted in such coarse, insulting language that Marxist translators and publishers have until now felt obliged to tone it down. Social critics of their caliber equated Ulrichs's effort with "converting smut into a theory." When they got into (admittedly remote) contact with important pioneers of sexual emancipation, they ignored or derided them. True, the question could not socially exist in the 1860s, but it was starting to be posed: Marx and Engels dismissed it and only bothered about the issue when it suited their political agenda.

But there is a bit more to it: "The infinite degradation in which man exists for himself is expressed in his relationship to woman as prey and servant of communal lust.... The immediate, natural, necessary relation of a human being to another is the relationship of man to woman." (Marx, "Private Property and Communism," in *Economic and Philosophical Manuscripts 1844*)

Engels *did* show an interest in sexual matters. In his 1883 article "The Book of Revelation" (in *Progress*, a magazine published by Edward Aveling, Eleanor Marx's partner), he wrote: "It is a curious fact that with every great revolutionary movement the question of 'free love' comes into the foreground." And his *Origin of the Family, Private Property and the State* is an in-depth critique of monogamy and woman's subjugation. Still, in the same book, Engels twice rejects (male) same-sex love, disdaining the Ancient Greeks' "abominable practice of boy-love" and the Black Sea steppes nomads' "gross, unnatural vices."

Marx and Engels perceived human exploitation and alienation not just in the "economic" domain, but also within sex relations… except for them sexuality only existed as "hetero"—a word and notion unknown to them. Therefore, in the name of the emancipation of both man and woman, they ignored—or in Engels' case repeatedly denigrated—what was coming to be known as homosexuality.

No More Greek Love

Like many others, when using the word *pederast*, Marx and Engels did not distinguish boy-lovers from adult "pederasts." This is one of the words that suffers most from layers of century-old confusion. In Ancient Greece, *paederestia* was a mode of socialization, a particular elder/youth relation that included sex but was more than sex, not opposed to marriage but complementing it. "In classical Athens … sex did not express inward dispositions or inclinations so much as it served to position social actors in the places assigned to them." (David Halperin)

History and ethnology tell us about the infinite variety of man-man sexual relationships that go far beyond what we now call "sexuality." Be it traditional adult and teenage male fellatio in New Guinea or communal life habits between young and older men, which our twenty-first century would call "homosocial," bordering on the "homoerotic." In these cases and a host of others, participants did not engage in "sexual practice." What happened was part of initiation rites necessary to reach the stage of ("heterosexual," in our modern mindset) masculinity, to become fully a "man," that is, a father and a warrior or a hunter (or both), and in Ancient Greece, a citizen. Where we might see "homosexuality" or "bisexuality" in the physical intercourse between *erastes* and *eromenos*, the citizen of Athens saw an entry into true masculine adulthood. After that, such an activity was to be avoided, and "passive" sexuality was frowned upon when practiced on an adult citizen.

We'wha had lived in a pivotal era, at a time when the birth of a "sexual question" lay the foundation for the coming of "homosexuality," first theorized and actually given a *name* by its pioneer defenders. Some men called themselves "homosexuals" in reaction to abusive and scornful terms applied to them. Oscar Wilde's lover, Lord Alfred Douglas, was behind his time in 1894 when he wrote about "love that dare not speak its name": by then, homosex had started to speak for itself and claim its legitimate existence on the scientific grounds that it was "natural." This was more than a vindication of rights on behalf of freedom. It was an effort to compete with established science by inventing new elaborate "progressive" models and sexual types against regressive rigid patterns. Inevitably, venturing onto the terrain of science led defenders of same-sex love to imitate its approach and methods; they soon categorized, divided, and subdivided sexual behavior, hoping to disarm hostile miscomprehension by accumulating solid evidence and exhaustive concepts.

❧

For homosexuality to exist as such, sexuality needed to be thought of and treated as a distinct social object. By creating "sexuality" as a specific sphere, capitalist society opened the way to a parallel: homosex and heterosex invented each other as reciprocal poles. Between the two, it was hardly a fair game: normativity was on the side of heterosex, because only heterosexuality appeared able to ensure the sexual order necessary to social reproduction. "At a time when the middle class sought to establish social order in the face of rapid industrialization and immigration, the control of sexuality outside of the family seemed all the more pressing.... Sex divorced from reproduction was simply too disturbing to unleash in public." (John D'Emilio and Estelle Freedman)

Law and morality continued to condemn homosexuality.

CHAPTER 3

What Is "A Man"? Of *Fairies* and *Men* in New York

Saloons and Drag Balls

In New York, at the end of the nineteenth century and in the first decades of the twentieth, men having sexual relationships with men did not separate this activity from their social life. They partook of a street culture, mainly working-class, in areas where blacks and Irish, German, Italian, and Jewish immigrants lived and worked in industry and commerce, the port and dockland particularly. Quite a few of those proletarians were male migrants, rootless, homeless, sometimes ex-convicts, with no marriage or family bonds. New York was a business and industrial metropolis, but it was also to a large extent a city of men.

The laboring classes' social life took place less in cramped and uncomfortable lodgings than in public spaces, repeatedly denounced by moral guardians and police as a threat to law and order. Homos made full use of that space. They lived in a popular environment, and their socialization took after it: saloons doubled as social centers or homes where they could find information, entertainment, a job, a partner, and in that sense they fulfilled the same function for them as for the rest of the neighborhood population. Besides, the same saloons would generally welcome homos and non-homos.

Within this lower-class urban life, the homosexual had a place. This is not to say that the New York working class was exceptionally sexually open and tolerant, but because of their specific material conditions of existence proletarians were not subject to and accustomed to the same "regulatory mode" of mores as the middle and upper classes: the differences in family, habitat, street habits, education, schooling, community, etc. created a very different separation between private and public spheres.

A peculiar feature of lower-class neighborhoods was the public visibility of the *fairy*: a man with so-called effeminate looks and manners. People were not indifferent to the possibility that he had sexual relations with male partners, but that fact was not essential. The man dressed like a woman or behaving as a woman supposedly does was a familiar figure in those neighborhoods and fairly well accepted, even to the point of being welcome in "normal" dancehalls, as well as starring in masquerades and drag balls, where fairies were the main attraction.

In Harlem in the 1920s, the Hamilton Lodge fancy dress ball was the biggest meeting event for same-sex-loving New York men and women; it gathered thousands of transvestites, mostly working-class, more so in the 1930s with an even stronger homosexual presence. In 1929, there were two thousand dancers and three thousand spectators, mainly young black workers. Attendance rose to eight thousand in 1937 and included many men in women's clothing, as well as women in men's clothing.

An eccentric fringe of "high society"—artists and socialites came as if to an offbeat fashion event—watching homos having a good time *voluntarily* making a show of themselves. The paradox of this stage-setting is that cross-dressing mocked the stereotype of the "unmanly" homosexual, while *perpetuating* it by presenting it as caricature. Carnival plays with moral patterns and social ranks: order is overturned for one night. The spectacle of inversion coexisted with the norm. While it highlighted the artificiality of sex roles, the fairies' outrageous femininity also reinforced female stereotypes.

Drag balls gave a primitive Eden (possibly tinged with racism) to quirky whites who could get away for a night from middle-class conventions, yet they also provided black and white gays and lesbians with a real party time and meeting place. There had been similar subcultures before, in Venice and Florence in Renaissance times, in eighteenth-century London, and places similar to the Hamilton Lodge existed in 1930s London and Paris, but on a much smaller scale and with less public presence. Nowhere was there such an open gay and lesbian culture as in those few decades in New York.

"I Am No Woman"

The fairy behaved as no "normal" man would but as any "normally" virile man would want a woman to behave.

The working-class neighborhood accepted—or at least put up with—the fairy as an anomaly more amusing than repulsive. Far from threatening the sexual hierarchy, the fairy was something else, an incomplete man and an impossible woman. Worse still, his/her display of femininity and disregard for such traditional feminine virtues as reserve and modesty made the fairy look like a prostitute.

From clothes choice to street gestures, feminization was the key criterion. "Non-normality" first lay in renouncing privileges and obligations typical of the status of a man, and only secondarily in looking for male sex/love partners. As for the man who agreed to the fairy's sexual advances, he was not considered "abnormal," as long as he stuck to what supposedly defines masculinity. This is why men, single or not, married or unmarried, living in immigrant communities with a high degree of segregation and hierarchy between the sexes, could be known to engage in regular same-sex intercourse without losing their "manly" status.

This was amply demonstrated in a famous 1919 trial. As it wished to wipe "sodomy" out of its Newport base, the US Navy selected in its own ranks a dozen young men chosen for their attractiveness, who were asked to seduce gay sailors in order to bring them to court. The "love trap" resulted in seventeen convictions. According to their testimonies, the sailors used as bait had no qualms about having sex with men who for them were not real men, only effeminate beings with whom they were the ones playing the true masculine role. (Let's not forget what John Howard later called "the unspoken rule of manly impenetrability." Manhood equals being active: "penetrated partners [were] more readily marked as queer than penetrative partners.")

In those days, a sexual partner's gender was not yet a decisive—and discriminating—criterion, but it was going to become one, the division between fairy and "real" man giving way to the demarcation between homo and hetero—a differentiation that appeared earlier in the middle and upper classes than among proletarians.

Class Distinction and Attraction

In the United States, exclusive heterosexuality was a necessary condition of "normalcy" in the better-off social strata, two generations before this became the case with black and white working people.

In the first decades of the twentieth century, the situation and income of middle-class men allowed them a private domain larger than the one affordable by male proletarians. The "well-mannered" man had the means to conform to the discretion and self-control norms that ruled his milieu, maybe to play the gentleman or even mix in with artists. If he preferred men, he could not and must not show it, so he disconnected his preference from his social image.

The fairy displayed his sexual difference in a vulgar way, i.e., as common people do: the educated man wore an elegant mask and often lived his same-sex affairs behind the façade of a conventional heterosexual couple. Sex markers also indicated social distinctions.

Appearance and respectability are part of the conditions of existence and work of the middle and bourgeois classes: clothes, speech, attitude, and body language are distinct signs of superiority that go together with their supervising and command role. In the 1930s, "a man is good-looking if he is well dressed," says a character in a recent novel by Alan Hollinghurst. Manners are a social passport. The school head does not talk like his kitchen staff, and if many workers aspire to respectability, few have the means to reach it. The man who can afford his own lovenest or a decent hotel room will always be better at keeping up appearances, in "classical" hetero adultery as in homophile love.

The worker proved his virility by playing the "masculine role" *with a man* as he also did at other times *with a woman*. The middle-class man, on the contrary, self-represented his virility as depending on an *exclusive* attraction to women. When working-class attitudes moved closer to those of the middle classes, this was another step in the moralization of the world of labor that had started in the nineteenth century.

Object Choice

"The very possibility of framing homosexuality as a site of identity and ethnicity presupposes sexual object-choice as a master category of sexual and self-identity."
—Steven Seidman, 1993, quoted by John Howard

How did this pattern gradually become predominant?

First, homo or hetero relations outside of marriage were a lot more common in the working class than in the middle classes.

Second, in the first half of the twentieth century, there was a major change in scientific discourse regarding the definition of sex roles. Until then, sexual *desire* was deemed less important than *the way* ("active" or "passive," particularly) desire was satisfied: the *invert*, sort of a man in reverse as the word suggests, was the man who acted like a woman, and to avoid inversion it was enough for man to play the dominant (active) role.

From then on, to be "a man," it was not enough to act like a man (i.e., *not to act like a woman*); it was also necessary to have intercourse *only with women*. Freud theorized this evolution by differentiating the *aim* (what sexual libido looks for, not necessarily intercourse in the usual sense but penetration, for example) from the *object* (how to obtain satisfaction by, among other things, the choice of a partner). Psychiatry kept on talking about inversion, but its most modern practitioners would rather theorize *homo*sexuality, defined as the attraction for the *same* sex, irrespective of the ways a man could "have sex" with another man.

It took a while for science to have a real effect on common behavior, because "biopolitics" is a lot more than a matter of writings and lectures. It was only after 1945 that a new perception of sexuality gradually won the day, thanks to its diffusion by welfare social services, public health bodies, and multiple media channels.

Besides—and this is more than an aside—sexual practices would not have changed without a deep transformation of the female condition, and, therefore, of the woman/man image, because of the tendency to equalize—partially and in a contradictory way—male and female conditions.

Most precapitalist societies confine the woman to specific functions that force a separate status upon her, usually as a secondary and minor social player. As it puts women to work outside the home, and now increasingly in "men's" jobs and tasks, modern wage labor does not eliminate but reduces the sexual hierarchy. In today's prevailing Western mental makeup, the woman has ceased to be perceived as a passive stay-at-home, indispensable but inferior to the active man who performs "real" work and is the family breadwinner. Logically, if the woman is no longer systematically subordinated to the man, acting like a woman is or was supposed to act becomes less of a symbol and a synonym for inferiority. Here the "(same)sex question" crosses paths with the more general question of the man/woman relationship.

This evolution was necessary for a historical reality called heterosexuality to arrive and coexist in a senior partnership with a parallel reality called homosexuality. In 1948, Professor Alfred Kinsey made it known to his incredulous fellow citizens that over one-third of US males had at least one experience of a sexual relationship with another male to the point of orgasm. When the "Kinsey Report" came out, its method and ulterior motives were questioned, but its large readership and the media reception showed that the times they were a-changin' (not just attitudes to same-sex love: Kinsey gave "shocking" rates of non-normative behavior, for example, both men and women's attraction to sado-masochism).

Lower-Class Rough Edges

"Manliness" differed in different social milieus. Freud's "civilized morality" was mainly middle-class morality, essential to middle-class self-definition. Because the workers' movement could be perceived as a threat to bourgeois law and order, the supposedly loose working-class morals were simultaneously repulsive and attractive to respectable society. Until the 1940s, the urban prole was the favorite partner of the English upper-class homo. The boss masters the worker's body in the factory. Oscar Wilde would buy the *rent boy*'s masculinity as the bourgeois bought the worker's labor power. The rented youth (he had to be young) gave the wealthy homo what the privileged missed: manual power, mastery over matter, the ability to be active by direct contact with things. In the workshop, the worker brings his physical strength and submits it to the boss's command; the sex for money relation was not dissimilar.

[T]he biological sex of the man's sexual partner mattered little but his position in the relationship a lot. He was expected to be assertive, tough, aggressive and even brutal, and his attitude underlay both his "active" penetration of the unmanly "queer" and his acts of homophobic assault and robbery: both confirmed his reputation as a real man. (Yuriy Zikratyy)

In his *Memoirs*, John Addington Symonds (1840–1893), art critic and advocate of "male love," described a "graffito" he saw in one of London's "sordid streets": "an emblematic diagram of phallic meeting" with the words "prick to prick so sweet," which to him expressed "so thoroughly the voice of vice and passion in the proletariat." Men from the elite called their young lower-class lovers "rough trade": both words are significant. "Feasting with panthers" was Wilde's encoded phrase for dangerous sex—less a risk of assault than of blackmail, in fact.

In the US too, there was a taste for working-class men: black writer and closeted homosexual Willard Motley wrote in a 1940 short story: "It is in the lower class for all its apparent rough edges, that the true warmth and vigor are to be found in the modern world." In the 1960s, the attraction for "the unmentionable, the workman in the donkey jacket" (Alan Hollinghurst) was still a cliché among middle-class London gays.

Very different was the (long socially and self-repressed) homosexual Daniel Guérin (1904–1988), who came from a bourgeois background to socialism and anarchism. In 1972, however, looking back on his youth, this is how he described his attraction to male workers:

Their way of life simplified to the extreme, their picturesque and male costume, their freedom of language, sometimes for me somehow undecipherable, their complexion tanned by the open air, their muscular vigor, their frank and natural animality that in those days neither factitious inhibition nor petit-bourgeois prejudice hindered or withered ... everything about them surprised me, metamorphosed me, enchanted me.

❧

Among the New York working class at the dawn of the twentieth century, heterosexuality as we know it was not an indispensable condition "to be a man." A man's desire for another man revealed as much and as little about his sex life as his preference for slim or buxom women.

A homosexual man was a man who behaved like a woman (was supposed to). Except at that time people did not speak of "*homo*sexuals," a word that only became common when the criterion shifted to "same sex/other sex." Today, a homosexual is a man who makes love to another man and probably lives in a couple with a man like man-woman couples, parenting included.

A while ago, stereotyped and caricatured homosexuality was the openly displayed fairy's femininity. Now, with body culture (and cult), the image of the deliberately masculine man prevails. Drag, provocation, and outrage are celebrated as fun at party time. There's no Gay Pride without them, but transgression comes second to the real thing, to going to the gym where the gay like many of his contemporaries cultivates his muscular masculine "body capital" (on the job market, best to be fit and athletic looking: "health is the new wealth").

Nowadays, sexuality is distributed on a homo-hetero axis, everyone being one or the other, possibly both at different times, the bisexual moving from one pole to the other, the queer combining ad lib variations, the transgender person crossing the biological limits that define (used to define?) each respective pole. As we will see in later chapters, at the end of the twentieth century, the hetero/homo binarism barely had time to assert itself before multiplying and dividing endlessly.

CHAPTER 4

Sexual Engineering in Moscow

The Russian Revolution was more than seizure of power, civil war, expropriations, etc.; it invented icons, symbols, a different calendar, new words in new combinations, and brought with it altered sexual parameters.

Before the Revolution

We can only regard individuals as "homosexuals" if they belong to a social context where this word is relevant for them and for society as a whole. In Russia, a male same-sex subculture emerged after the 1870s, and a female one in the 1890s. The word "homosexual" only arose in Russian in 1895, becoming part of educated speech after 1905. Even after that, many people who had same-sex relations rarely called themselves "homosexuals."

Before 1917, "there was little identification with a specific group of 'one's own people,' with an effeminate self-image or with an exclusive sexual orientation. Individuals in positions of authority indulged in same-sex erotic acts for pleasure, while their subordinates apparently acquiesced with a view to material if not personal profit." (Dan Healey)

This does not imply that it was socially indifferent or well accepted. In any case, there was more "bisexuality" than is generally supposed today, but without the concept, because same-sex love was a practice among men with a family life. For a "modern homosexual subculture" to emerge, it required capitalist modernization and all that entails (mass urbanization, in particular). It was only then that some people started to regard themselves as a group: "our own kind," different from those who exploit a public image of normative masculinity, who dress like women, who sell themselves, or all three at once. "Sex in public was an affirmation of the self." (Dan Healey)

Bolshevik Cross-Dressing

> It was ... rumoured that Kerensky liked to dress in women's clothes. There was much that was rather feminine in Kerensky's physique and gesture. ([Zinaida] Gippius called him her "girlish revolutionary"), and this made him appear weak to many of the workers, in particular, who contrasted him unfavorably with the muscular masculinity of the Bolsheviks.
>
> —Orlando Figes

We will leave it to Orlando and Zinaida—symbolist poet, 1869–1945, and a friend of Kerensky's—to decide what is feminine and masculine, but their opinions reflect a certain state of mind, at the time and even now.

By any standard, Red October was definitely virile. After 1917, a lot of women adopted "masculine-style" behavior and clothes, at least in urban centers. The Bolshevik woman took on masculine attitudes and looks to the point of what might have appeared as caricature. The correct political code for both sexes was to be soldier-like, and equality of the sexes hardly went beyond that. Instead of submitting to masculine domination, woman activists were subjected to the party and the state, and history records very few woman leaders in the party, the state organs, or the Comintern. Alexandra Kollontai was the exception that proved the rule.

Some women took advantage of this dress style and attitude to engage in inter-woman love, albeit cautiously—as cover. Until the mid-1930s return to traditional values, the regime turned a blind eye on covert lesbians who played the part women were expected to play in socialist Russia. Energy, determination, toughness, and self-sacrifice were promoted among women as among men. Against bourgeois codes but in favor of work and politics—the party line, that was. Some women who took an active part in the revolution, as well as some lesbians, had the opportunity to assert themselves as women, which echoed the principle of equality, one of the main planks of the regime. This also buttressed a still fragile regime that had to mobilize all available human energy.

Socialist Biopol

In pre-1917 Russia, a strong movement, also active in socialist circles, was in favor of turning sexuality into a private matter, in the name of individual freedom. When in power, however, the Bolsheviks favored a scientific-bureaucratic vision of society: rationalization as opposed to emancipation, collective (re)production rather than personal liberty—everything for the common good, as understood by the party and as beneficial to the workers' state.

The good party cadre was one who was able to turn into an efficient factory manager. As for the grassroots proletarian, he/she was the ideal Soviet man or woman, the developer of the productive forces "for the purpose of properly distributing and rationalizing all social labor," as Lenin wrote in 1914. Therefore, breeding future workers is as much of a socialist step forward as building a new tractor plant, and, in fact, the two were inseparable.

The Bolsheviks wished to do away with the inward-looking family unit, hypocritical moral double standards, and the closed-in couple, because "communist morality demands all for the collective." While making it clear in 1921 that "all sexual relationships must be based on mutual inclination, love, infatuation or passion," Kollontai stressed the fact that the bonds between the members of the collective must be strengthened…. The needs and interests of the individual must be subordinated to the interests and aims of the collective. On the one hand, therefore, the bonds of family and marriage must be weakened, and on the other, men and women need to be educated in solidarity and the subordination of the will of the individual to the will of the collective…. The stronger the ties between the members of the collective, as a whole, the less the need to reinforce marital relations." (The word *collective* is repeated forty times in a 3,160-word text.)

Consequently, if sex is social, society has the right and duty to regulate it. Regarding same-sex love, it is telling that Kollontai, the famous advocate of "sexual freedom" and "free love"—in theory, as well as in her own eventful life—never spoke publicly in favor of homosexuality. In inner party circles, everyone knew that Chicherin (commissar for foreign affairs, 1918–1930) was gay, but this was accepted as long as he kept quiet about it, which he did.

Inasmuch as it supervised the grain harvest or steel production, the socialist state oversaw social reproduction, which by definition includes procreation. This was far more important than Lenin's often quoted dismissive remarks, as reported, for example, by Clara Zetkin: "Promiscuity in sexual matters is bourgeois. It is a sign of degeneration. The proletariat is a rising class. It does not need an intoxicant to stupefy or stimulate it, neither the intoxicant of sexual laxity or of alcohol."

Bolshevik systematic policymaking was one of the strongest historical attempts to apply the rule of science (as befitted the party), to do away with religious beliefs, and to create secular state morals with limited means. Homosexuality is a perversion, not a perversity, a young

Russian psychiatrist said in 1922, and should be treated in hospital, not penalized. The new state gave itself the monopoly on distinguishing between normal and pathological. On a materialist basis, sexuality is a "superstructure," the theory went: what is bad is whatever distracts men and women from productive activity, from work, from party activism. Unlike the idle parasitic bourgeois, the proletarian works: that was the nub of the new positive morality. What does not contribute to (re)production, the Bolsheviks averred, is antisocial and anti-socialist. Therefore, reproductive (man + woman) sex is "proletarian," whereas same-sex love is "bourgeois." In that period, homosexuality was still only indirectly repressed, because it deviated from social duties, not in itself. Until 1934, no sexual act was banned unless committed with underage or vulnerable people. At the time, "unnatural" acts could send someone to prison in Germany, as could "buggery" in Britain.

Like in other countries, Soviet science debated the "causes" of homosexuality. One school of thought argued in favor of biological, natural yet changeable, determinants: nature was amenable to nurture. Homosex was caused by hormonal anomalies, so it could be cured by adequate treatment. Another current insisted on biosocial causes. Sometimes the two viewpoints converged.

Sexual Order

With the first Five-Year Plan (1928–1932; 1932 because it was supposedly fulfilled in four years) and the tightening of state control, traditional family values were deemed more compatible with order and policing than the (*very relative*) sexual emancipation possible after 1917, and a better fit with a pronatalist policy: abortion was made illegal in 1936 and remained so until 1955.

Same-sex love was increasingly treated as a religious, rural, feudal, precapitalist—and, therefore, anti-socialist—remnant, especially at the periphery of the USSR, in the

Muslim and Caucasus republics. A "cultural revolution" was launched in the name of modernization vs. archaism. For party officials and activists, the cultural was political, and nothing was natural, so no "third sex" theory, no endocrinal factors: homosexuality was amalgamated with pedophilia in anti-church propaganda and court action. Militant atheism denounced homosex as a particularly vicious form of exploitation of man by man.

In contrast, authentic proletarians, typified by Russian workers, were said to have sound and healthy mores, as opposed to the backward peoples in the East; Uzbekistan and Turkmenistan had a tradition of brothels with young males, and Bolshevik legislation banned them at the same time as polygamy, forced marriage, and dowries were banned. The Uzbek 1926 code outlawed "sexual harassment of men" (just as the 1923 Russian code outlawed it for women).

All these elements were to conflate with the repressive Stalinist legal system. Women were most welcome in the workplace (and in the army, according to Russian tradition) and could perform men's tasks, as long as they also played their part as mothers in the family.

After 1929, not unlike Foucault's seventeenth-century "great confinement," Russian policy was to bring together all elements unfit for productive labor (prostitutes, the homeless, vagrants, beggars, alcoholics, sex deviants, and those involved in "unofficial" informal street trades) and forcibly reeducate them into proper workers. Homosexuals no longer belonged in the hospital but in the labor camp. Anomaly was not a moral issue, only a social (to avoid work) and political (to evade statist control) issue. The "workers' state" was treating the issue as a class question: homosexuals were work shirkers at the best, bourgeois saboteurs at the worst. Homosexuality had been decriminalized after 1917 but recriminalized in 1934.

One step further, Gorki justified anti-homosex policy in the name of anti-fascist struggle. Fascism, he explained, mobilized youth in order to neutralize its revolutionary potential, particularly by practicing and promoting homosexuality. Thereby fascism sterilized proletarian energy. (Our next chapter will return to this.) So homosexuals were not simply immoral; they were enemies of the people, pure and simple. Therefore, "destroy homosexuals—fascism will disappear," the writer demanded.

"To Dear Comrade Stalin"

In May 1934, Harry Whyte, a twenty-seven-year-old, who had been a member of the Communist Party of Great Britain since 1931, was living in Russia, where he edited the *Moscow Daily News*. Singled out as the "best shock worker," Harry was no dissident, except in one field. He wrote Stalin a four thousand–word letter to prove that the new "anti-sodomy" policy of the USSR "contradicted both the facts of life itself and the principles of Marxism-Leninism." Carefully separating the private from the public spheres, he methodically made his Marxist point on scientific, as well as political, grounds and left no doubt about his interest in the subject:

> I have a personal stake in this question insofar as I am a homosexual myself.... I contacted the OGPU [political police, ex-Cheka, later NKVD and finally KGB] in connection with the arrest of a certain person with whom I had had homosexual relations. I was told there that there was nothing that incriminated me.
>
> ... I view the condition of homosexuals who are either of working-class origin or workers themselves to be analogous to the condition of women under the capitalist regime and the coloured races who are oppressed by imperialism. This condition is likewise similar in many ways to the condition of the Jews under Hitler's dictatorship, and in general it is not hard to see in it an analogy with the condition of any

social stratum subjected to exploitation and persecution under capitalist domination.

As he put it:

[T]here are two types of homosexuals: first, those who are the way they are from birth (moreover, if scientists disagree about the precise reasons for this, then there is no disagreement that certain deep-seated reasons do exist); second, there are homosexuals who had a normal sexual life but later became homosexuals, sometimes out of viciousness, sometimes out of economic considerations.

Ultimately, he argued, the solution

is the revolutionary transformation of the existing order and the creation of a society in which the absence of unemployment, the growing prosperity of the masses, and the liquidation of the family as an economic unit [in order to] secure the conditions in which no one will be forced into pederasty out of necessity. As for so-called constitutional homosexuals, as insignificant percentage of the population they are incapable of threatening the birth rate in the socialist state.

In sum, he fully agreed with arresting homosexuals for "reasons of a political nature" but said there was no need to prosecute anyone *merely* because he was a homosexual. Same-sex love was neither a medical abnormality nor a danger to socialism.

Though the letter argued "in accordance with the principles of Marxism-Leninism," Stalin never answered; he just left a note calling Whyte "an idiot and a degenerate."

A lone voice, Harry Whyte left Russia in the mid-1930s (and so avoided being eliminated in the Great Purge), later drifting away from Stalinist communism but remaining left-wing and dying in Istanbul in 1960, leaving an estate of £1 to his Turkish partner, or so the story goes.

The 1960 revised Soviet Criminal Code punished consensual sex between adult men by up to five years in prison. This was repealed in 1993 but, as we know, contemporary Russia continues to persecute homosexuals, often in the name of protecting minors from "gay propaganda": the ever-watchful state enjoys nothing more than defending what it regards as pure and innocent youth.

CHAPTER 5

Sexual Reform in Berlin

Germany was the first country with sizeable, established, and lasting homosexual organizations, until Nazism wiped them out. It is no exaggeration to point out the connection between this movement and the social explosions and insurrectionary attempts that shook Germany between 1919 and 1921. The first phenomenon did not have a direct effect on the second, but they were linked.

A Social Movement

There was a homosex milieu in New York, but in Germany, it had the breadth and depth of a social movement, which resonated with a lot of people in all walks of life, so much so that Harry Kessler, homosexual writer and art collector, noted in his diary on November 8, 1907: "It's insupportable, even little girls on the tram are discussing homosexuality."

This was a world of difference from Britain, where pro-homosexuality public campaigning was unthinkable. Ulrichs would have been unpublishable in a country that banned Havelock Ellis's *Sexual Inversion* (1897), a scientific book by a renowned scholar. In Germany, only "blatant pornography" was prosecuted, banned, or censored. This also differed from France, where same-sex love was not criminalized, but where there was little "scientific" interest in or publication about the subject.

A whiff of decadence clings to pre-1933 Berlin's gloomy and naughty "sexual freedom," as portrayed in the film

Cabaret (1972), inspired by Christopher Isherwood's auto-biographical fiction. Image and myth mask the reality of same-sex love—between both men and women—on the eve of World War I. Before 1914, there were about forty Berlin homo bars, mostly with a middle-class clientele but also in working-class neighborhoods. An observer in a workers' district tavern reported: "They slave away during the entire week so they can enjoy a Sunday evening indulging their tendencies.... And when they go to the voting booth, they vote as workers, always and without exception—Social Democratic." A majority of Berlin men in same-sex relationships were working-class and were often "integrated into their immediate neighbourhood." (Robert Beachy) Significantly, contrary to London, blackmailed homosexuals did not hesitate to turn to the police.

In 1903, Magnus Hirschfeld's Scientific-Humanitarian Committee (discussed in the next paragraph) sent a questionnaire to three thousand students, and a year later to five thousand metal workers, asking them about their sexual orientation, with four possible answers: preference for women, for men, for both, plus a fourth option, "deviation," for those who chose not to identify with of any of the other options. Apart from four students who successfully sued Hirschfeld, the survey was positively received. The proportion of self-declared homos was similar in the two social groups; 1.5 percent among students, 1.15 percent among workers, with 4.5 percent "bisexuals" among students and 3.19 percent among workers.

After 1918, a number of same-sex bars and dance halls were used as meeting places, sports clubs, and conference halls, in a humanist and pacifist mood, always with a mind to repealing § 175 of the Criminal Code: "Unnatural fornication, whether between persons of the male sex or of humans with beasts, is punished with imprisonment." Other bars functioned as informal social centers comparable to New York saloons. In the rest of the country, every mid-size town had several homo bars and meeting places, under various names ("friendship centers," "clubs"), and each was usually home to the local branches of nationwide organizations, which, however, had little influence in rural areas and rarely included both men and woman. This sociability contributed to the circulation of a thriving "homo press," as diverse as the rest of the media: some magazines similar to popular mags, some illustrated, others aiming at an "educated" audience, sometimes with a political leaning but usually politically neutral.

The Deutsche Freundschaft (German Association of Friends) had 2,500 members in 1922. With a membership of 12,000 in 1924 and 48,000 in 1929 (including 1,500 women), the Bund für Menschenrecht (BfM; Human Rights Federation) came close to being a mass organization. Extrapolating from data collected by the Scientific-Humanitarian Committee, the BfM reckoned there would be as many as two million homos in Germany in the mid-1920s (out of a total population of sixty-three million). Based on these findings, the BfM described homosexuals as respectable citizens who fully deserved to be integrated into German society and rejected the minority within the minority, especially the most visually transgressive "fairies" and male prostitutes. To achieve its goal, the BfM thought it realistic to appeal to the goodwill of all political parties... even the Nazis.

Most progressive German defenders of same-sex love justified their demonstration on the rights of *nature*: homosexuality was innate, and from birth some men experienced an irresistible attraction to the same sex. Though this line of reasoning was not unanimous (the BfM disapproved), it was widely accepted, because it seemed a better policy to present homosex as "an inborn condition" (which is what many of today's gays say). If it had been a question of freedom, i.e., a matter of choice, homosexuals could have been held responsible for their "unnatural" behavior.

Magnus Hirschfeld (1868–1935), in particular, took up and expounded the theory of a "third sex": some men were driven by congenital psychological factors toward an original sexual orientation. He was the main founder, in 1897, and leading figure of the Scientific-Humanitarian Committee (SHC). Based in Berlin, the SHC had subcommittees in other large towns and organized lectures and conferences for the most varied audiences: elite all-male clubs, businessman associations, student organizations, etc. For mass meetings, it rented "class-appropriate" locations in working-class Moabit, "large enough to host an audience of a thousand or more" (Robert Beachy). In 1919, the SHC developed into the broader Institute for Sexual Science (ISS). Its Berlin premises combined reform activity (supporting the suppression of § 175), scholarly research, popular education, and medical consultations (3,500 in 1919–1920: two-thirds of the patients were men, one-third homosexuals). Hirschfeld was intensely active, traveling, lecturing, initiating debates, and, in 1919, he inspired what was likely the first openly pro-homosexuality film, *Different from the Others* (featuring Conrad Veidt, a famous actor who a year later played the leading role in the expressionist classic *The Cabinet of Dr. Caligari*). Initially successful, the film was soon banned from public screening and only shown to private audiences.

As indicated by the wordings—Scientific-Humanitarian, Sexual Science—and the motto adopted by the ISS—"through science to justice"—the idea was to scientifically, i.e., by politically-neutral irrefutable methods, provide same-sex love with the legitimacy that would guarantee its public recognition and allow its social existence. Hirschfeld was a believer in "biological determinism" (R. Beachy) as it was conceived of in his time. By measuring skulls (criminals' skulls especially), nineteenth-century doctors would draw patterns of behavior (and deviance). Likewise, Hirschfeld thought homosexuals often had larger hips. He looked for categories. He created names, and, in 1910, coined the word *transvestite*. He also compiled and archived a treasure trove of objects, testimonies, surveys, and pictures, most lost when the Nazis ransacked the Berlin premises in 1933. This encyclopedic turn of mind was part of a trend to collect and anthologize items and documents on people's ways, customs, and folklore: the institute wanted to complement "elite" erotic art with sexual science to prove the extreme variety of sexuality, as well as the contribution of homosexuals to civilization and culture.

The committee and its successor institute would gather up to one thousand participants from all social classes in their conferences and debates. They also had local groups, some in working-class neighborhoods that met in Moabit beer cellars.

Politically, the SHC, in 1897, and thirty years later the ISS, vainly petitioned against § 175, despite support from thousands of intellectuals and artists, plus a few political figures: Franz Wedekind, Stefan Zweig, Hermann Hesse, Thomas Mann, Sigmund Freud, Richard von Krafft-Ebing, Albert Einstein, Eduard Bernstein, August Bebel, Karl Kautsky, and the theologian Martin Buber (playwright Wedekind authored *Pandora's Box*, which inspired Georg Wilhelm Pabst's 1929 film *Loulou*, with Louise Brooks, an icon of the new "sexually free" woman, who also played with a bisexual image).

The Nazis made the law worse by broadening it to include whoever the police wanted to harass and prosecute. Ten to fifteen thousand homosexuals died in the concentration camps.

After the war, § 175 remained as it had been before 1933, leading to tens of thousands of convictions (in that matter, dictatorial East Germany was slightly more lenient than the democratic West). Nearly all prosecution under § 175 stopped in the late 1950s, but it took another couple of decades for the anti-homosex law to be fully repealed, both in West and East Germany, and for the age of consent to be gradually lowered for males.

The Political Uses of Same-Sex Love, Act 1: Imperial Germany

Before 1914 and in the Weimar Republic, homosex was a "political question" in Germany, which was not the case in the US, Britain, or France. The growth and persistence of such a large political homosexual movement (political in the sense that it went with collective self-defense and pressure on legislation) as the one that existed in Germany, on a scale unknown anywhere else, could not fail to attract the attention of political parties, especially those dedicated to reform, the socialist SPD, and later the communist-Stalinist KPD.

August Bebel (1840–1913) is now less remembered as the leader of the SPD in the pre-1914 period than as the author of *Woman and Socialism*, first published in 1879, several times updated by the author, often reprinted, and for a long time the most read "Marxist classic" on the subject. Bebel says little about same-sex love, except that in Ancient Greece misogyny and fear of overpopulation led men to keep away from women and have "unnatural" relations among them- selves. Same-sex love is also treated as an "aberration" for women.

By the time he updated later editions, Bebel had read Hirschfeld (who had befriended Bebel while still a student) and he had come to regard homosexuality as an "inborn" condition—therefore, part of nature—but in the 1910 edition "sodomy" remained a "perversity" for men and women alike. In fact, Bebel, apparently haunted by "the Greek Age" (like Engels, as seen in chapter 2), tended to view homosexuality as a by-product of the subjection of women in ancient times, and probably in his own.

In contrast, while Oscar Wilde was being tried at the Old Bailey in 1895, Eduard Bernstein emphasized the relativity of mores and morals and questioned the basis of an accusation against homosexuality:

Although the theme of sexual behavior may not be of paramount significance for the economic and political struggle of social-democracy, the search for an objective means of assessing this side of social life as well is not irrelevant. It is necessary to discard judgements based on more or less arbitrary moral concepts in favor of a point of view deriving from scientific experience. The Party is strong enough today to influence the shape of State law, its speakers and its press influence both public opinion and members and their contacts...

For what is not unnatural? Our entire cultural existence, our mode of life from morning to night is a constant offence against nature, against the original preconditions of our existence. If it was only a question of what was natural, then the worst sexual excess would be no more objectionable than, say, writing a letter—for conducting social intercourse through the medium of the written word is far further removed from nature than any way as yet known of satisfying the sexual urge.

The epitome of reformism, Bernstein stood for evolutionary change. He was more of a humanist than a communist. Maybe this is what helped him sympathize with the plight of human beings persecuted not on grounds of class but solely for their sexual leaning, an issue that most of his revolutionary critics dismissed as "bourgeois."

As we have seen, two years later, Bebel, Bernstein, and Kautsky signed the SHC petition against § 175. Homosexual rights were becoming a progressive cause worthy of support, which also meant a minor but not to be utterly neglected source of votes. Being a workers' party did not prevent the SPD from asserting itself as a people's party capable of appealing to many social groups.

In the Reichstag, on January 13, 1898, Bebel spoke in favor of suppressing § 175, mainly for practical reasons: "The number of these people is so great and reaches so far into all levels of society" that the vice squad could not cope with it; § 175 was unjust but above all unenforceable and obsolescent. Unlike Bernstein, Bebel did not inquire into the heart of the matter, and his words sound rather tame by contemporary standards, but he was well in advance of his time. This was most likely the first speech in any parliament in which a high-level leader of a party, one that was a model for socialists all over Europe, took such a stand.

However, if the growing relevance of the question forced parties to take a position, it also allowed them to capitalize on the matter when it benefited their political agenda.

The SPD exploited "sex scandals" when it saw fit. In 1902, its central organ *Vorwärts* was one of the first newspaper to "reveal" that the arch-bourgeois Friedrich Alfred Krupp allegedly had relationships with underage boys in Capri; a few weeks later, Krupp committed suicide.

In 1906–1909, the SPD took the same approach to another class enemy, a close friend of the emperor's, Philipp zu Eulenburg, also accused of homosexuality. The affair resulted in a succession of high-profile libel suits and confused court actions involving members of the military high command, all the way up to Chancellor Bernhard von Bülow. In the accusations and polemics that ensued, the socialist press stood by accepted public morality. "There are two points on which the different parties will always agree: when it comes to interfering with private life and when it is possible to express one's moral indignation." (Franz Pfemfert)

A number of anarchists (and homosexuals) denounced these methods. Senna Hoy (1882–1914), for example, refused to treat homosexuality as a propaganda tool that could be used in one way or the other, saying that exploiting these affairs was "an indecent weapon." (Senna Hoy was to die in a Russian jail, where he was imprisoned in 1907.) "So the question is how far you are justified in using a prejudice that you don't share to destroy a political opponent, and to be sure, not simply politically, but utterly and totally." (Harry Kessler's diary, October 29, 1907) True, but in all likelihood socialist journalists *also shared anti-homosexual prejudices*.

The Political Uses of Same-Sex Love, Act 2: Weimar Republic

After the empire fell, the political and social climate was favorable to reforms, and the SPD wielded considerable power. It was a major partner in all but one of the Weimar coalitions, and three chancellors were SPD members. Though the repeal of § 175 was still officially part of its program, the SPD had lost interest in the homosexual cause: a ruling party is respectful of public morals.

The KPD (communist party), which was only in office for a few weeks in Saxony and Thuringia in 1923, had less need to preserve an image of respectability. In 1924, it presented a motion in parliament calling for § 175 to be repealed; by a turn of events, the government fell, and there was no vote, so the matter was dropped. On May 16, 1927, Wilhelm Koenen spoke in favor of legislative change on the matter; he was the only KPD MP to force the issue in parliamentary debate. The party press and statements took a more determined stand than those of the SPD, and KPD members participated in the activities of the Scientific-Humanitarian Committee. Richard Linsert (1889–1933), for example, became secretary of the SHC in 1923. One of the KPD's main legal experts, Felix Halle (born in 1884, and shot in Russia as "a counter-revolutionary" in 1937) published *Sexual Life and Penal Law* (1931): "The working class, far from cultivating same-sex inclinations and activities … takes a tolerant approach toward such manifestations of sexual life."

Inevitably, the SHC was politically divided. Hirschfeld, a pro-SPD moderate, hoped for reform from above. A more "radical" wing, represented by Linsert and Halle, insisted on linking sexual questions with overall social change (as understood by KPD members in a Leninist party on a fast road to Stalinization). For instance, they refused to limit depenalization to "honorable" homosexuals (i.e., those who kept quiet about it). When, in 1929, the SPD introduced a bill to legalize homosex but with a higher age of consent and the criminalization of male prostitution, the SHC split, and Hirschfeld left the organization. Parliament never adopted the law, and the 1929 crisis plus the rise of the Nazi Party swept the issue aside.

All the while, the KPD did not hesitate to exploit sex scandals. In 1924, its press branded "serial killer" Fritz Haarmaan a homosexual. In 1932, it attacked same-sex love as a "bourgeois vice" as evil as prostitution, sadomasochism, and bestiality. But it was against the self-declared homosexual Brown Shirts' leader Ernst Röhm that the most lurid reports were unleashed: KPD's journalists and orators counterposed sound healthy proletarian sex to fascist decadent depravity. Of course, Röhm was a Nazi and head of the SA thugs, but, above all, he was presented as a degenerate and, therefore, an ideal focus for hatred: he fit the bogeyman monster stereotype. In 1930, the KPD was acting in the same way the SPD had toward Krupp in 1902. When an enemy's alleged or avowed homosexuality serves as a pretext to attack him, this amounts to targeting homosexuality.

The most infamous aspect of this policy was illustrated by the KPD's treatment of Marinus van der Lubbe, the young Dutch council communist who set fire to the Reichstag on February 27, 1933. Stalinists accused him of being an agent provocateur in the pay of the Nazis and made much of the fact that he was homosexual. Such was the official version propagated in nineteen languages by the *Brown Book of the Hitler Terror and the Burning of the Reichstag*. Van der Lubbe was even portrayed as Röhm's *Lustknabe*, meaning a sexual partner and often a prostitute. In the ensuing trial, van der Lubbe's Stalinist codefendants demanded he should be sentenced to death for having "worked against the proletariat." He was executed; they were acquitted. A year later, in his letter to Stalin mentioned in the previous chapter, Harry Whyte wrote about "fascism, which employed the pederast van der Lubbe as a weapon in its provocation."

Neither the elimination of Röhm and the SA's leadership in June 1934 nor the merciless anti-homosexual Nazi policy in December immediately put an end to the equation: "homo = degenerate = Nazi = enemy of the people." Anti-fascist propaganda even traced down hidden homos among the high-up Nazi leaders and made fun of "Frau Hitler."

Not many voices were raised against this line of conduct. As expected, the Scientific-Humanitarian Committee was highly critical. So was Kurt Tucholsky's left-wing weekly *Die Weltbühne*. Linsert refused to be part of "sexual accusation" (he died on February 3, 1933, so he never knew about van der Lubbe). In *The Left and "Vice"* (1934, also known as *Homosexuality and Fascism*), Klaus Mann refuted the fallacy that "fascist Röhm was homosexual, therefore, homosexuality is fascist" and wrote against Gorki's ferocious anti-homosexual article mentioned in our previous chapter:

> Homosexuality is not to be "extirpated," and if it were, humankind would come out impoverished of something incomparable.... The meaning of the new humanism, for the realization of which we want to see socialism as a prerequisite, can only be in one thing: tolerating not only all that is human and which does not cause criminal troubles in the community, but integrating it, loving it, making it accepted, so that the community benefits from it.

The aggravation of legal and extrajudicial repression of homosexuals in Germany finally forced anti-Nazi propaganda to shift gears, but the bias remained, in accordance with Wilhelm Reich's fascist "emotional plague" concept. (In his fight for sexual freedom, Reich believed that same-sex love resulted from our sexual misery and would wither away when we could enjoy an unfettered and rewarding sex life). Granted, most Nazis leaders were not homosexuals, and same-sex love was outlawed in Nazi Germany, but, the Reichian theory goes, the fascist individual is often a self-repressed homo; Nazism won over the masses by addressing their affective (sexual, particularly) dissatisfaction and mobilized its activists by providing them with a substitute male community (with a strong sexual component, though it was not openly acted out).

Against fascist ideology that availed itself of nature, health, vitality, and energy, anti-fascism turned the argument around by "psychiatrizing" the enemy: the fascist is the unhealthy one, constrained, self-repressed, and just like the "invert" is his own prisoner. Not all homosexuals are fascists, yet homosexuality is one of the high roads to fascism.

Reich's classic *Mass Psychology of Fascism* was written between 1930 and 1933. After 1945, the linkage between sexual ambiguity and fascism (and/or sadism) would long remain part of received wisdom, illustrated, for example, in two famous artistic works: Rossellini's *Rome, Open City* (1945) shows a (most unpleasant) German lesbian and an effeminate Gestapo officer; Moravia's novel *The Conformist* (1951, filmed by Bertolucci in 1970) describes how troubled (homosexual-tinged) sex leads to fascism.

Looking back, these attitudes adopted between the two world wars do not differ much from those of nineteenth-century socialists summed up in chapter 2. In 1930, as in 1900 or 1864, sexuality and "homosexuality" were rarely taken into account—or simply taken seriously—for what they were, but only as political tools to be used between competing parties—convenient for accusation and gossip.

Identity Overload

In 1945, Magnus Hirschfeld (who lived in exile after the Nazi takeover) had been buried in Nice for ten years.

Starting from four primary criteria based, according to him, on an inborn biological infrastructure, and then recombined and subdivided according to each individual physiology, libido, and subjectivity, the tireless sexologist had concluded that there existed an immense range of sexual possibilities: forty-three million variants, no less.

What can we make of a forty-three-million-rich identification? Any identity implies some kind of limit that circumscribes it and gives a minimum of homogeneity that differentiates it from neighboring identities. What consistency can exist in a kaleidoscopic whole fragmented into a near-infinite interplay of factors? And why forty-three million? Why not forty-two? Or forty-nine? There may be doubts about the "scientific" relevance of such an improbable inventory. Let us, rather, take it as an intuition as insightful as those of Fourier when he classified his harmonic series, his 810 characters, his 12 + 1 passions methodically divided into sub-passions, etc. Hirschfeld's merit is not his accurate calculation of the number of love orientations and permutations. He simply drew his contemporaries' attention—and ours—to the impossibility of fencing the universality of sexual life within mental, let alone legal, boundaries.

CHAPTER 6

Butch/Fem, or the Rise and Decline of the Woman Worker Image

Butch and fem. Or is it butch *versus* fem? This mode of sexual and emotional relationship between women has often been an object of ridicule, scorn, and scandal, and certain feminists reject it as a caricatured mimicking of heterosexual codes, as if one woman was playing the masculine role and her partner the feminine one. In fact, there is more to it than a domination game, and butch/fem also has a class dimension.

Best to hear the people concerned speak for themselves. Elisabeth Lapovsky-Kennedy and Madeline Davis interviewed women involved in this milieu in Buffalo, New York, from the end of the 1930s to the 1960s. According to these historians, oral history has to be given priority, because most of the participants were working-class and left no written testimony.

Homes and Bars

In those days, Buffalo was an industrial town where many people had jobs in car factories and steel mills.

In the US as a whole, the proportion of women in the working population rose from 27 percent to 37 percent between 1940 and 1945, and one married woman out of four worked outside home, which gave her more autonomy and, for those with a husband in the army, more opportunities to meet new people. For a woman attracted to other women, however, there was a risk of being exposed as "deviant" and losing her job, so she had to compartmentalize her private and public lives. A lesbian who worked in a factory from 1936 to

1966 said she was always discreet about her sexual orientation: what she could do as a teenager was forbidden to an adult.

In the 1940s, bars (often also functioning as entertainment halls) opened in Buffalo, which (mainly because it was good business) aimed at a mixed clientele of blacks, whites, gays, lesbians, and heteros, as well as call girls and petty offenders.

Of course, Buffalo's lesbianism was not limited to bars. The Daughters of Bilitis, one of the first organizations dedicated to lesbian liberation in the US, founded in 1955 and active in the Buffalo area, had middle-class members who did not patronize places they regarded as vulgar and uselessly provocative. On the contrary, for most working-class lesbians, bar culture was the linchpin of social life. When home is de-emphasized, bars are the main socializing place. These women gave few home parties and had no family life and very little couple life: friendships were fragile, and stable relationships rare. Most of them did not go back home to a partner when they left the bar. "The defensive stance and the related competition for lovers and for positions of control did not encourage the vulnerability necessary for intimate friendships." (This and all subsequent related quotes are from Lapovsky-Kennedy and Madeline Davis.)

Gays and lesbians seem to have mingled, with "no ideological commitment to separatism." In 1993, an interviewee said about the 1940s: "We were never segregated like they are now. There was never a question about a gay guys' bar. We always went to the same bars, this is how we got to know so many gay bars."

Let's not romanticize. There was competition, aggressiveness, even violence between lesbians and straights, and sometimes between lesbians. One had to conquer one's space: "the bars were our only territory. It was exciting when the prospect arose to occupy a new territory," Tony remembered. "It wasn't like, 'OK, I'm queer, so now I'll get on with my life and become something wonderful.' Being a butch meant I was limited if it was only for how I dressed, what I looked like. I was already an outcast." There was fighting for space in bars and areas that were rough and were not respectable. All the more so, given that, "In general, prostitution was an accepted occupation for fems, although the community was not altogether free from self-righteous judgment."

Polarity and Sex

All narrators "agree that butch-fem roles predominated in the public lesbian community of the past." Originally, *butch* indicated a tough-looking and tough-acting man, preferably big and virile. In choosing the word, some women wished to take on the clothes and attitudes of the most dominant masculine image.

"As in most places, butch-fem roles not only shaped the lesbian image but also lesbian desire, constituting the basis for a deeply satisfying erotic system.... [T]hey were at the core of the community's culture, consciousness, and identity. For many women, their identity was in fact butch or fem, rather than gay or lesbian."

"Butch and fem mannerisms were modeled on male-female behavior as portrayed in the Hollywood movies of the period." It went with a way of walking, sitting, holding a cigarette, pitching one's tone of voice: "Most butches were expert mimics who had mastered the subtleties of masculine non-verbal communication." They imitated rockers' "careless and tense" style and favored men's clothes, specifically work clothes. As for the fems, they were dedicated followers of fashion and familiar with Hollywood actresses' attire. "[G]ender polarity pervaded the whole culture and was therefore difficult to escape." Two butches could be friends, never lovers. The same applied to two fems. Leather hardly mixed with lace. This replicated the binary model. Whatever personal feelings these women may have had about the "butch/fem code," whether they thought it was inborn or acquired, natural or artificial, they had to abide by its rules: "They were a social imperative [in order to] participate comfortably in the community and receive its benefits." This may be difficult for us to admit in an age when roles are regarded as a personal choice, but, back then, peer social pressure was accepted and, according to Lapovsky-Kennedy and Madeline Davis, it helped build a community.

Sexually, "lesbian sexual culture was based on the eroticization of the difference between masculine and feminine": "the butch was expected to be the doer and the giver." The butch was supposed to be the active partner, the fem the passive one: in butch/fem lovemaking (the most common form of sexual practice was what they called "friction"), the fem did not "reciprocate." Oral sex was uncommon, and there was neither much innovation nor sex toys. Many lesbians who started as butches in the 1940s stayed butches, yet fems tended to swap roles more easily.

In other words, a woman-centered, albeit gender-defined erotic system.

Reappropriation and Internalization

Using stereotypes did not imply copying traditional couples— no more than New York fairies pretended or wished to appear as women. The purpose of playing a masculine role was not to pass as a man but to intensify his image, to caricature it.

Lapovsky-Kennedy and Madeline Davis interpret this playing with norms as a "pre-political form of resistance": before lesbians could publicly exist, recreating male over female domination with an all-female cast was a way of crossing the gender line, and it bonded women: "The solidarity offered tremendous support in a society which was hostile to lesbians." According to these historians (who are also lesbian rights activists), the butch/fem impersonation permitted three forms of resistance: it helped lesbians assert themselves in a hostile world; it decreased the private/public divide; and it physically and visibly defended a woman's right to love another woman.

Not everyone agrees. Some feminists argue that making fun of social patterns (particularly age-old sexist ones that weigh so heavily on women's condition) does not subvert them; it perpetuates them, and, thereby, plays in the hands of the enemy. Mimicking masculine tropes objectifies women, critics contend; in social struggles, parody and travesty are double-edged swords, at the best.

The question will be left open for the moment. Let us just note that there was something desperately ironic in the butch enacting a role model that in real life was oppressing her (like a prisoner pretending to be the jailer). When the stage was bare and the butch left the bar, she could not continue to play that part or could only do so at her own risk.

Class

Contrary to the long tradition of "explicitly trans-class" erotic gay socialization, the lesbian bar clientele has a strong social "homogeneity"; most of the patrons came from a "working-class lesbian community," and middle-class women tended to keep away, for fear of tarnishing their social image. (*Working-class* meaning woman factory workers, but also bus drivers, typists, shop assistants, switchboard operators, hospital staff, hairdressers, postal workers, cleaners, all poorly paid female jobs, usually manual and mostly unskilled.)

Butches who worked in factories generally did not display any singularity in the workplace, but they would wear working clothes when going out at night. Besides, for those butches employed in the service sector, dressing like a manual worker enabled them to affirm in the evening a "proletarian" style that they were forbidden to adopt during the day. Both blue- and white-collar lesbians partook of the valorization of the male proletarian. As we saw in chapter 3, in the first half of the twentieth century, high-society homos would look for a virile lover among sailors and stevedores. The working class was a symbol of enduring strength, as well as a challenge, a possible threat, which made it more ambiguously desirable. "The butch-fem image typified and reproduced the class distinctions within the lesbian community and was central to shaping and expressing their politics."

A survey of lesbian life in Montréal confirms the class pattern observed in Buffalo: "in the 1950s and 1960s, there was no homogenous lesbian culture, only sub-cultures defined by social class: working-class lesbians had different ways of recognizing each other." (Line Chamberland) Montréal women interviewed have strikingly opposed memories. They all agree in describing the bars as a "rough and violent milieu where the toughest imposed their own rules." But middle-class lesbians remember the drinking, the excess; they depict butches as if they were not authentic lesbians and the fems as women who reproduced hetero codes. On the other hand, lesbians from a working-class background say they felt comfortable with that milieu and insist on the plus side: love and sex, solidarity, and a gratifying self-image.

Sure enough, working-class lesbians' lives were different. Underage boys and girls would illegally frequent bars, the butch was a well-known presence in those neighborhoods, and parents would warn their daughter against going too near her. Butches often had "men's" jobs (transport, warehouse work, taxi-driving) that did not subject them to the same discretion as prevailed in middle-class professions.

From Rosie to Role-Play

All sexual imagery draws upon the mental images that predominate in a certain period. The butch/fem duality adopted the positive view of the male American worker in those days, and its female counterpart symbolized by the mythic "Rosie the Riveter." A government-sponsored 1943 poster showed a bandana-wearing woman in blue overalls flexing her muscles and looking at us saying "We Can Do It!": women were up to manufacturing the weapons the men were using to win the war.

There was reality in the myth. The poster was quite probably inspired by a picture of Naomi Parker Fraley (1921–2018), photographed in 1942 while working at California's Alameda Naval Air Station. (Actually, despite her bandana and work clothes, Naomi cut a not so obviously muscular figure: she looked less like a shock worker than a model. The real Rosie was more fem than the butch poster Rosie.)

Joining the workforce in traditional masculine jobs gave women a newfound sense of selfhood. By 1944, three million women made up 22 percent of all trade-union membership in the US. Lesbian behavior and representation adapted to the evolution in feminine images.

A couple of decades later, as elsewhere in North America, industry has decreased in Buffalo, and the urban population with it: 580,000 in 1950, 350,000 in 1980, 260,000 in 2010. When worker reality declines, its imagery withers: the bandana is cool, but the blue overalls are out-of-date. Ways and habits have changed. In this day and age, you see fewer stiletto heels in the street and more pants than in 1960. The growth of feminism and homosexual (mainly male) self-assertion has transformed the perception of lesbianism, which in some circles is even treated more as a political movement than a sexual practice.

The evolution brought about its own contradictions, and feminism, always a diverse and fractious alliance, became less of a front than a battleground. In Buffalo, as in the rest of the United States, one might have expected a rising feminist movement to integrate lesbians, but making common cause did not prove straightforward. Middle-class feminists mostly asked for legal changes, feminists engaged in the labor world focused on job and wage equality, and black feminists fought against the combination of racism and sexism. For quite a while, far from converging, feminists and lesbians had tumultuous relations, fueled by denunciations and bitter feuds, and the 1970s and 1980s *sex wars* were even worse for the butch/fem milieu, which found itself being shot at from both sides.

On the one hand, majority feminism, under the influence of white middle-class people looking for integration, could hardly associate with such an obviously disrespectable crowd. When you wish to be socially accepted, you tend to keep away from those who break away from norms. Some feminists called for legal censorship against "degrading" pornography and even denounced S and M "sexist" practices, and being labeled "sex positive" or "pro-sex" was enough to get you stigmatized as "objective allies" of male oppressors, a sort of enemy within.

Besides, not only were they turned down by mainstream feminism, but butch/fem adepts were also ostracized by a lot of radical feminists, who accused them of replicating stereotypes essential to masculine domination: playing a man's part was playing the enemy's game. In 1984, Joan Nestle, born in 1940 and involved in the New York working-class butch/fem bar culture and a gay and lesbian activist, wrote about the "irony of social change": what appeared in the 1950s as "sexually and politically radical" came twenty years later to be regarded as "reactionary and non-feminist." Her explanation: for women on the way to hard-won social promotion, the butch/fem image "characterized and reproduced class distinctions within the lesbian community." Needless to say, butch/fem was no class *action*, it was mimicry and role-play (according to Joan Nestle, more permutation occurred than is commonly believed), but even *that* was unpalatable to consensus-seeking feminism and unacceptable to moralizing radical feminism.

Time has passed. The woman who played at being a worker in the evening (whether or not she was one during the day) found herself out of place with a real women's movement in the working world fighting for labor *and women's* rights on the shop floor and in the office. In the US today, four in ten families have a female main income earner, and this part of the working class (in the broad sense) has started getting organized, outside and—increasingly—inside union structures. The long tradition of union neglect of woman labor has started to change, partly thanks to women's empowerment and partly because declining organized labor needs all the rank and file it can get. The "Rosie the Riveter" imagery has become a standard at union marches and on posters, expanded to embrace a variation of muscle-displaying bandana-wearing black, ageing, or even deliberately sexy woman workers.

Meanwhile, in a smaller sex scene, it persists as role-play, albeit often with a shift in representation: worker's—i.e., male workers' clothing is now less important in butch paraphernalia than it used to be. For a butch today, it's projecting "masculine" *behavior* that matters.

CHAPTER 7

"To Be What We Do Not Know Yet": Stonewall and Aftermath

At the end of the 1960s, homosexual self-defense erupted into an explosive fire and glare that included an attempt at global social critique. When the momentum subsided, rebellion became merely self-assertion: gays increasingly fought as a group, asking for public and legal recognition. Some people, however, did not resign to the inevitable. This chapter will be limited to significant moments in three countries: the United States, France, and Italy.

From Urban Riot to "Gay Power"

For a police raid to turn into a riot, it took a strife-ridden time: workplace insubordination, strikes of a new type, as in the General Motors Lordstown plant, black riots, civil rights marches, and anti–Vietnam War mobilization. The "homosexual liberation" movement was not the direct result of class conflicts, but its dynamism was closely linked to the 1960s–1970s proletarian revolt: the impetus came from the lower classes.

In New York City's Greenwich Village, the Stonewall Inn had a mixed clientele of poor white, black, and Latino gays. Like many similar bars, it was owned by the mafia, and its manager Fat Tony would regularly pay off the cops, which did not prevent regular police raids like the one on June 28, 1969, except that this one met with fierce resistance.

The cops were used to being shouted at and booed, but a turning point was created when a "cross-dressed butch lesbian" (arrested for violating a New York edict that required each person to be wearing three pieces of "gender-appropriate" clothing) struggled against being pushed into the wagon. A Puerto Rican construction worker threw a cobblestone at the police car, people in the crowd slashed all four tires, the cops left the wagon unattended, the prisoners escaped, and by then the whole street was erupting. The raiding squad barricaded themselves in the now empty Stonewall, the door was smashed, petrol bombs exploded inside, the officer in charge was ready to shoot, then the riot squad arrived. Unrest continued the next night, and three days later widespread violent street fighting resumed.

Many rioters were poor or homeless young gays, some of them waifs and strays living on a knife's edge of subsistence, a multinational, multiracial crowd, and "the most marginal groups of the gay community fought the hardest—and therefore risked the most—on this and the following nights." (David Carter)

The revolt reverberated, the protest swelled into mass action, which drew in reformers, as well as radical left groups. Some formal organizing appeared, with slogans like "gay power" and "equality for homosexuals." Unlike previous movements that merely asked for tolerance, gays and lesbians now wanted immediate full equality for all sexual orientations. In that respect, they stood in solidarity with the civil rights movement, and 1969 was a watershed year. When a rioter said, "I was part of a mob that had a kind of deep identity," that commonality was a lot more than sexual. Those who affirmed themselves as gays thought they were part of an oppressed community that would converge with other similar communities into a unified "people" so vast and strong it could set everyone free. A week after Stonewall, the Gay Liberation Front (GLF) was founded, advocating "Power to the People!"

Unlike a party, a front provisionally aggregates diverging interests around the priority of a common goal. But GLF members weren't much concerned with the exact meaning of the word, rather, they ideologically identified with national liberation fronts in the Third World, especially in Vietnam.

In 1970, the Radical Caucus program declared:

> We see the persecution of homosexuality as part of a general attempt to oppress all minorities and keep them powerless.... A common struggle, however, will bring common triumph. Therefore we declare our support as homosexuals and bisexuals for the struggles of the Black, the feminist, the Spanish-American, the Indian, the Hippie, the Young, the Student, and other victims of oppression and prejudice.

The idea was to assemble all those categories into a "people." (In general, these activists did not expect much from the worker—the white one, at least—whom they usually regarded as a chauvinistic sexist reactionary.)

Because of the disparate and opposed interests of this multilayered people, the popular front was bound to fail, causing a succession of splits in the GLF. A "left-wing" fringe wanted a broad revolutionary agenda in solidarity with other oppressed minorities. The "moderate" majority focused on demanding sexual equality—for example, fighting against gays being banned from federal jobs. The rift was inevitable, and realistic pragmatism finally carried the day.

There was a visible gap between those like the Stonewall rioters, who had the least to lose and the most to gain from fighting back, and those who favored not rocking the boat. The former lost; the latter won: they got some seats in the boat. Because bourgeois rule and state power were challenged but not overthrown, the social surge was eventually (in fact, quite quickly) diverted into democratic demands parallel to those of the huge civil rights mobilization.

The underdogs who had initiated the revolt identified with the worldwide downtrodden, which was how they saw them, in any case—the Viet Cong trooper, the Palestinian guerrilla, the Third World freedom fighter, the black, the woman…—and hoped for the unity of the oppressed and a revolutionary outcome. When that failed, they were swept away, and there was only room for identifying with a presumably more accessible identity: the gay world, expanded later into the LGBT+ world.

"Gay Power to Gay People": "We shall aggressively promote the use of the very real and potent economic power of Gay people throughout this land in order to further the interests of the homosexual community…. We will not be gay bourgeoisie" (*Come Out*" no. 1, November 1969)

Despite this disclaimer, if you want "very real and potent economic power" in this capitalist society, best be a bourgeois. The first sentence has some grip on reality. The second is ideology. "Gay power" was utopian, and utopias fail as utopias—and succeed as institutions—when they imitate the world they initially rejected.

"We'll Be Gay until Everyone Has Forgotten That It's an Issue"

Born in 1943, Carl Wittman wrote *Refugees from Amerika: A Gay Manifesto* (1969, published the following year by the Gay Liberation Front), soon to become a point of reference.

The title is to be read literally: more than a mere statement, a manifesto intends to express a group's collective experience and strategy, in this case a minority forced into a ghetto, "out of self-protection":

> We are refugees from Amerika. So we came to the ghetto—and as other ghettos, it has its negative and positive aspects. Refugee camps are better than what preceded them, or people never would have come. But they are still enslaving, if only that we are limited to being ourselves there and only there. Ghettos

breed self-hatred. We stagnate here, accepting the status quo.... It is a ghetto rather than a free territory because it is still theirs. Straight cops patrol us, straight legislators govern us, straight employers keep us in line, straight money exploits us. We have pretended everything is OK, because we haven't been able to see how to change it—we've been afraid.

What homosexuality is: Nature leaves undefined the object of sexual desire. The gender of that object is imposed socially. Humans originally made homosexuality taboo because they needed every bit of energy to produce and raise children: survival of species was a priority....

Bisexuality is good; it is the capacity to love people of either sex. The reason so few of us are bisexual is because society made such a big stink about homosexuality that we got forced into seeing ourselves as either straight or non-straight.... We continue to call ourselves homosexual, not bisexual, even if we do make it with the opposite sex also, because saying 'Oh, I'm Bi' is a copy out for a gay. We get told it's OK to sleep with guys as long as we sleep with women, too, and that's still putting homosexuality down. We'll be gay until everyone has forgotten that it's an issue. Then we'll begin to be complete.

About "Alternatives to Marriage," Carl Wittman wrote:

People want to get married for lots of good reasons, although marriage won't often meet those needs or desires. We're all looking for security, a flow of love, and a feeling of belonging and being needed. These needs can be met through a number of social relationships and living situations.... We have to define for ourselves a new pluralistic, role free social structure for ourselves. It must contain both the freedom and physical space for people to live alone, live together for a while, live together for a long time, either as couples or in larger numbers; and the ability to flow easily from one of these states to another as our needs change.

The *Manifesto* was unconcerned by one of the main reasons why gays and lesbians have fought for same-sex marriage since 1969, and, finally, in many countries have won the right to marry: the possibility of joint ownership and transmitting a legacy to your partner. Neither renting or buying a flat nor heritage were relevant for Carl, because he thought society was on the cusp of overall change. If you are convinced that the time will soon come when no one will risk being a vulnerable individual, there is no need to resort to (bourgeois) institutions to protect us, for example, by giving marriage and coownership rights to stable and durable same-sex couples. In a future society without money and property, dying intestate would be meaningless, and, in 1969, tomorrow seemed not far away.

In the eyes of Carl Wittman, this approaching society would not promote stable durable couples, be they homo or hetero, but would favor our "ability to flow easily" from one sexual option to another. In stark contrast to the "born that way" argument put forth by homophile activists—in 1969, and even more so now—Wittman believed everyone had the capacity to love both men and women. He issued a wake-up call to "free the homosexual in everyone," while also suggesting that "gays will begin to turn on to women ... when women's liberation changes the nature of heterosexual relationships."

When ill with AIDS, Carl Wittman declined hospital treatment and committed suicide by drug overdose at home in 1986.

Exploding Sexual Codes

In 1970, the Front Homosexuel d'Action Révolutionnaire (FHAR) was created in France by a group of women, with men joining them a couple of months later. "For the moment, homosexuality remains the common denominator for a set of oppressed individuals," and "coming out of the ghetto will depend both on the possible transformation of desire and on the global political fight of revolutionary forces.... For us, homosexuality is not a way of destroying society. It is first and foremost our situation, and society forces us to fight it." (*Report against Normality*, 1971)

While woman founders and participants expected a lot from a mixed-gender organization, the massive influx of men soon led to a prioritization of male homosexuality and hindered the group's activity. As a woman member later said: "I saw a completely changed FHAR.... Collectiveness had withered into factions.... In about a year, the fairies associated with the fairies, the gays with the gays, the dykes with the dykes, the politicians, the Marxists between themselves." ("Still a Woman Worker," *Gai Pied* no. 9, 1979)

Some lesbians reproached the FHAR for misogyny, split and created the *Gouines Rouges* (Red Dykes). In the FHAR, "Group 5" hoped to avoid ghettoization by collaborating with heterosexual far-left groups, and failed: "Our intention was ... to get across to leftist groups the idea of sexual liberation. We had to give up." For their part, the fairies rejected formal organization and hierarchy, called themselves *Gazolines*, adopted slogans like "proletarians of all countries, embrace!" and specialized in provocation, much to the displeasure of far-left activists, who were usually endowed with a poor sense of humor.

An informative but optimistic 1972 article in *Gulliver* described the FHAR as four thousand strong, with groups being founded "almost everywhere" in France and an international organization being born, largely on the mistaken belief that there was something inherently revolutionary about homosexuality. Guy Hocquenghem (1946–1988) was an eminent proponent of the theory that, with adequate strategy, FHAR could work as a catalyst for overall social change, a political outlook aptly described by Jeffrey Weeks in 1978 as "a worship of the excluded and the marginal as the real material of social transformation."

A minority of the FHAR opposed this view and insisted that, while there are revolutionary homos, there is no revolutionary homosexuality. They felt the organization was beginning to

> reconstitute a new kind of ghetto, in particular with the affirmation of a homosexual identity conceived of as revolutionary in itself, which could not be the case with bisexuality, downgraded as a recuperation: that was the opposite of a multi-sexuality or polysexuality which had been the founding stone of the FHAR and of our project. (Lola Miesseroff)

Indeed, what Lola and her friends had appreciated was that the FHAR was not pursuing "homosexual liberation" but bringing together homosexuals—plus a few others—for "revolutionary action," and they applied the same logic to the women's movement: "It is positive for groups to deal with specific issues, providing they are not destined to become permanent, providing they are meant to melt into the revolution, especially as the revolution was going to take place tomorrow." For them, therefore, a radical women's movement could not be a women-only organization.

The minority (composed of men, women, gays, lesbians, bisexuals, and heteros) who had joined the FHAR on the basis of "let's explode sexual codes" realized the organization was going exactly the other way, so they left and explained in a leaflet:

The emancipation of homosexuals will not be the work of homosexuals alone. The problem of homosexuality is only a partial aspect of the general problem of relations, which will be solved only in total transparency between individuals and the goal and means of the revolution. Nevertheless an organization of homosexuals is necessary: it is from the awareness of their specific oppression that their awareness of the general oppression of relationships can arise.... Because it is a specialized organization, the FHAR acts as a ghetto and breeds ghettos. We soon intend to meet with those outside the FHAR ghetto who already suffer from this state of things, and who wish for the FHAR to go beyond itself. We demand the total question of relationships to be posed, and solved in a way which can only be revolutionary.

As the FHAR had become unable to serve as a meeting structure "creative of new relations," the dissidents hoped this could be done by neighborhood committees, quite active in the immediate post-1968 years, and which, thanks to their local embeddedness, "could do away with the separation between activism and the rest of daily life."

Lola Miesseroff remembers:

In Paris, in the early 1970s, a group of about ten people settled in a three-room apartment: two bedrooms and a room where it was forbidden to sleep, because it was reserved for people who would spend the night talking. We stood for what was later called *polysexuality*. We used the word *pansexuality*, but we were neither zoophiles nor pedophiles, not any more than Sados or Masos. Other similar apartments were created, there was a free flow, everyone mingled, we had whole night discussions, we went to demos, always in a group, but not as a community, because there is impoverishment in a community. We were in a group to be active together. It was a time of extreme and intensive effervescence in ideas, discussions, actions and sex. And of course, our friends who were basically homos were particularly involved in the fight for the end of the repression of homosexuality. As we also took part in the fight against the repression of women.

A member of the FHAR known as Marlene, at that point a young man, said, in 1972, "What we want is the total transformation of life. One only makes revolution if one lives it permanently, in everyday life."

Quite, but how could this be achieved, when the tide of rebellion was ebbing? In the absence of multidimensional social dynamics, the various forms of critique were increasingly compartmentalized, contest was degraded into protest, and the abovementioned neighborhood committees were unable to reverse the process. While it aimed at destabilizing society and abolishing sexual normality, the FHAR died of being caught in the contradiction between the *vindication* and the *critique* of the homosexual subject. As in the US, French gays went from a demand for tolerance to the self-affirmation of a community to a call for recognition and rights. The dream soured, and the demise of the FHAR closed an era of revolt.

Le Fléau Social (The Social Plague) was launched in 1972 as the mouthpiece of dissidence within the FHAR (in 1960, the French parliament had added homosexuality to the list of "social plagues" like alcoholism, drug-taking, etc., hence the name). Soon Alain Fleig (1942–2012) became its editor and the main writer and opened up the magazine to unorthodox anarchism and Marxism, with a special interest in the situationists. A homosexual movement on the fast track to fragmentation crossed paths with a (deficient) communist movement. Sometimes *Le Fléau Social* sold rather well (over ten thousand copies), but the adventure ended with the fifth issue in 1974.

"Gay Communism"

Mario Mieli (1952–1983) was a high-profile figure in the homosexual movement in Italy, where, in 1972, he cofounded the radical gay magazine *Fuori* (Outside). He also lived for two years in London, traveled in Europe, and, in 1973, attended a few meetings of an ailing FHAR in Paris: "a general meeting of the FHAR is very beautiful if you live it as a trip, but it becomes rather frustrating if you go there … to get an idea of what French revolutionary homosexuals are up to."

To Mario, provocation and scandal were necessary to drive home the idea that there is no revolution without a reinvention of the use and meaning of our bodies.

In 1977, the year when social turbulence in Italy approached an insurrectionary threshold, he published *Homosexuality and Liberation: Elements of a Gay Critique*. Chapter titles said it all, from the first ("Homosexual Desire Is Universal") to the last ("Toward a Gay Communism").

Mario Mieli's notion of "transsexuality" is likely to have a disconcerting effect on the twenty-first-century reader:

> I shall use the term "trans-sexuality" throughout this book to refer to the infantile polymorphous and "undifferentiated" erotic disposition, which society suppresses and which, in adult life, every human being carries within him either in a latent state, or else confined in the depths of the unconscious under the yoke of repression. "Trans-sexuality" seems to me the best word for expressing, at one and the same time, both the plurality of the erotic tendencies and the original and deep hermaphroditism of every individual.

Regarding what is now known as transgenderism, he wrote:

> At the present time, these manifest transsexuals are still subject to the contradiction between the sexes and the repression of Eros, which is the repression of the universal trans-sexual (or polymorphous and hermaphrodite) disposition common to all human individuals. Persecuted by a society that cannot accept any confusion between the sexes, they frequently tend to reduce their effective trans-sexuality to an apparent monosexuality, seeking to identify with the opposite "normal" gender to their genital definition. Thus, a female transsexual feels herself a man, opting for the male gender role, while a male transsexual feels himself a woman. A human being of "imprecise" sex has a much harder time just getting around than does a male person who seems, by all external signs, to be a woman, or vice versa. This is why people who recognize themselves as transsexual in the present society often want to "change" (genital) sex by surgical operation, in Casablanca or Copenhagen, or rather more frequently, restrict themselves to strict psychological identification with the "opposite" sex.

This statement might qualify today as sheer indifference to the plight of transgender persons, or even as transphobia.

Therefore, "the liberation of Eros and the achievement of communism pass necessarily via the (re)conquest of trans-sexuality and the overcoming of heterosexuality as it presents itself today."

Mario was fully aware of the "recuperation" of same-sex struggles that was already under way in the 1970s:

> Today it is clear that our society makes very good use of the "perversions"; you need only go into a

newsagent or to the cinema to be made well aware of this. "Perversion" is sold both wholesale and retail, it is studied, classified, valued, marketed, accepted, discussed. It becomes a fashion, going in and out of style. It becomes culture, science, printed paper, money—if not, then who would publish this book?

Other voices expressed a similar concern. The same year as Mario's book, one could read in a Turin mag:

> I don't want to be recuperated by heterosexual normality because I do not believe in it. But I do not believe either in a homosexual model and then, as I am aware of my limits, I want to progress in my liberation in order to explode all that I have repressed…, I want to change myself and to be neither homosexual nor heterosexual, to be what we do not know yet, because it is repressed. (*Lambda* no. 2, 1977)

In those days, like Carl Wittman and the early FHAR members, Mario expected the advent of revolution (or at least an attempted one) in a fairly near future. When capitalist collapse did not happen in the 1970s, there was a shift in theory. Most of Mario's book elucidates how a communist movement and a revolution had to include the sexual dimension and the "gay" issue. Then, in the last chapter ("Toward a Gay Communism"), sexual matters become *the cause* of capitalist perpetuation, consequently sexual liberation becomes the lever that could move the capitalist world. The "complete disinhibition" of homoeroticism was previously described as "one of the conditions of the creation of communism": it is now turned into *the* condition, because monosexuality is thought of as the basis of capitalism.

"Today, the revolution is being prepared, among other things, by the conflict between the gay movement and the Norm, and by the encounter between homosexuals and deserters from the army of normality." (As the book goes on, more key words are capitalized, a sure sign of concepts receiving a life of their own and theory feeding on itself.)

The political culture that had acted as a disruptive force had had its day. As the proletariat—gays included—seemed to recede from the historical stage, Mario entered a headlong pursuit of other revolutionary subjects. He hoped "revolutionary lesbians" could serve as a bridge between the gay and feminist movements. Then, as too few revolutionary lesbians were up to the task, he believed in an increasingly large and more diffuse and dematerialized historical agent, so universal, in fact, that it exists everywhere and nowhere:

> True human subjectivity is not to be found in the personification of the thing par excellence, i.e., capital and the phallus, but rather in the subject position of women, homosexuals, children, blacks, "schizophrenics," old people, etc. to the power that exploits and oppresses them. This revolutionary or potentially revolutionary subjectivity arises from subjection.

Mario's impossible contradiction was wanting sexual revolution to be merely part of social revolution… while considering sex as the prime bearer of an invincible subversive power. He neither nurtured illusions on the ascending gay movement nor accepted defeat as the fighter for a "new (and very old at the same time) eroticism, polysexual and transsexual." Asking too much of one's epoch can lead to soft or hard self-destruction. Others tried to fan the flames of revolution after the fire had turned to ashes. When the setback proved permanent, Mario, lost in political limbo, took refuge in writing and in mysticism, until he killed himself at the age of thirty-one.

"There will never be satisfied revolutionaries." (*La Révolution Surréaliste* nos. 9–10, 1927)

AIDS and Self-Defense

A few years after Mario's death, the devastating AIDS epidemic contributed to transforming gay revolt into a movement for the defense of a category (in 2016, 1.7 million people worldwide died from tuberculosis, a million from HIV/AIDS, and half a million from malaria).

Though it is statistically more lethal among heteros (women, notably), AIDS led to a strong commitment on the part of homosexuals, paradoxically reinforced by the fact that the epidemic was initially associated with homosexuality: people spoke of "gay cancer," and it took years before the press stopped writing about "GRID" (Gay-Related Immune Deficiency) and started using the terms "HIV" and "AIDS."

When Act Up was founded in the US in 1987, the name was significant: Aids Coalition to Unleash the Power by direct action. On both sides of the Atlantic, Act Up went back to the 1970s radical methods: rejecting respectability, openly affirming a different sexuality, doing more than victim support, acting politically, confronting reactionary power (the Catholic Church, among others), street provocation, disturbing the media, and an effort—in the beginning, at least—to function without leaders, as a federation of autonomous collectives. The growing self-awareness and militancy of those who called themselves and were now called "the gays" helped change a public image; homosexuality was no longer—or not just—a sexual practice, it was looked as a way of life characteristic of a minority, possibly of a community.

Fighting AIDS and all established powers that cared little about it, be they medical, political, or media speeded up the creation of militant associations and support groups, some of which later gave birth to institutions that sometimes benefited from public funding. When defending a group's interests needs some degree of social recognition, it is logical that its support groups—Act Up included—should receive government or local authority grants and subsidies. Besides, if large sectors of public opinion and politicians remain hostile to same-sex love, the enlightened reformist wing of the bourgeoisie favors individual and collective empowerment, in sexual matters as in everything else; each minority is welcome to have its own morsel of power on its specific terrain, as long as it abides by global social rules: respect for the class system and deference to state authority. There now exists a homosexual "movement" that is not directly political but plays a political role on behalf of collective interests.

Gay and lesbian public legitimacy, media presence, institutional recognition, and involvement in administrative structures have gradually reached a stage unimaginable by 1970s radicals. Looking back, Jim Fouratt, Stonewall rioter and early member of the Gay Liberation Front, remembered that at the time he and his friends tried to make "a gay revolution" and "had no interest at all in being acceptable." About fifty years after Carl Wittman's *Manifesto*, few homosexuals wish to publish a statement announcing their intention to fight for total social change. Gays, lesbians, and bisexuals, as well as transgender and intersex persons, rarely deliver messages to the world. They claim their lawful rights.

CHAPTER 8

Impossible Identity

"As a Black lesbian feminist ... I find I am constantly being encouraged to pluck out some one aspect of myself and present this as the meaningful whole, eclipsing or denying the other parts of the self."

—Audre Lorde, 1980

Martha Shelley, when a member of the Gay Liberation Front, which was founded for gays and lesbians a few weeks after Stonewall, wrote that opposition to the nuclear family was a central tenet of sexual liberation activism. In 1970, another GLF member, Allen Young, stated that family was the principal means by which "restricted sexuality" is "created and enforced." They could hardly have imagined that fifty years later, gay and lesbian groups would fight for the right of gays and lesbians to have a family life.

The Contradiction of Integration

Gay revolt fuels radical critique when it disturbs, in small or large measure, the moral, social, and even racial order; for that reason, amid the 1960s–1970s turmoil, it contributed to a global social challenge.

Then the rebel surge began to look like a party that has gone on for too long and that was showing signs of ending soon. When the wave receded, homosexuals tried to fulfil their elementary claims by daily reform action, as well as through institutional channels, in order to consolidate a partial and fragile public and social acceptance. In 1997, the title of a collective book published in the US adequately summed up the gay and lesbian fight: *Creating a Place for Ourselves*. As gays and lesbians, they aimed at finding a place in society and at being included rather than shunned and ostracized.

Edmund White describes how the spontaneous gay refusal of marriage, which gays regarded as "another example of assimilation," has been replaced by a demand for the right to marry, the ultimate symbol of painstakingly obtained—and still contested—integration into society. Then, as the "man + man" or "woman + woman" couple proved as functional as the hetero couple—or certainly no more dysfunctional—and, therefore, a quite reliable basic social unit, it was logical and legitimate for same-sex couples to raise and adopt children. After being treated as abnormal, homos wish for a "normal" life.

Likewise, in 2016, quite a large number of gays and lesbians legitimately rejoiced at the official inauguration of the Stonewall National Monument in New York. A place formerly raided by police is now a protected area meant to honor a broad equality movement. US president Obama extolled "the richness and diversity and uniquely American spirit that has always defined us.... [W]e are stronger together.... [O]ut of many, we are one."

Radicals who bemoan the "integration" of the gay/lez movement miss the point. Same-sex love did not run out of a revolutionary zeal it never had or has; it is not subversive in itself, even if it has to resort to militant, violent, and unlawful action. A vast majority did not want to live in exile from their own society and aspired to a personal and collective self-betterment, which went with aligning with ameliorationist and gradualist politics.

As early as the 1970s, activists "spoke of fixed sexual orientations rather than polymorphous desires," and "what had been an underground sexual culture increasingly came to resemble an urban community." (John D'Emilio and Estelle Freedman)

Way of Life or Lifestyle?

"Homosexuality—and, by inference, heterosexuality—was no longer understood as a set of acts, but as an identity; not as behavior, but as a state of being."
—John Howard

Does this validate the existence of a *homosexual way of life?* At the most, there exists a *gay lifestyle* that concerns a minority of the homosexuals who assert a distinct sociability. The bare fact is that their micro-society is but a micro-culture that revolves around meeting places, leisure, shopping, shared cultural references, and gay-run businesses. In the US, the National Gay and Lesbian Chamber of Commerce, founded in 2002, is "the business voice of the LGBT community" (1.4 million LGBT business owners), which certifies over one thousand LGBT enterprises. "Business ownership thrives in the LGBT community because we have all learned to be the entrepreneurs of our own lives," says one of the cofounders.

Undoubtedly, despite the disparity in education, position, and income, the gay doctor, the lesbian soldier, the gay delivery man, and the lesbian manager all share, to a different degree, discrimination due to their sexuality, if only because of the obligation to hide it or be discreet about it. In countries like France or the US, anti-homosexual hostility is still active and coexists with a growing social acceptance. Hence a tension between homos who want "to belong" and some activists and businesspeople who try and maintain what they have in common.

But being a victim is not enough to spawn a community, no more than a sexual disposition is enough to define mores. Community means sharing an origin or special social bonds or a religious faith or converging essential interests or usually a combination of several of these elements. Sexual orientation does not create belonging.

There is no "gay society." LGBT *activist* media may be very active, but there is next to no gay or lesbian press (printed or on-line) comparable to the abundance of magazines on every possible subject. The lefty gay reads the *Guardian*, while the lesbian football fan watches her favorite sports channel.

Once the common sexual difference is socially accepted (even to a limited extent), social hierarchy reasserts itself: the gay boss acts like a boss and his gay employee like an employee, and they will only take to the street together on Gay Pride day or for a demo in support of same-sex marriage. When the Paris Gay Pride organizers do their utmost to prevent the FLAG's float (FLAG being the gay and lesbian police officers' organization) from coming too close to the anarchist float, what sort of community is that? Sydney Gay Priders are more relaxed: at the week-long Mardi Gras festival—one of the largest such events in the world—gay and lesbian cops just add a rainbow flag or scarf to their uniform, and they police a crowd that takes hardly any notice.

To borrow Carl Wittman's words, "straight cops," "straight legislators," "straight employers," and "straight money" are now complemented by "gay cops," "gay legislators," "gay employers," and "gay money."

When same-sex love was legally and socially repressed, homo sociability was first of all sexual, and that dimension determined the rest. In New York, "gay men built social ties on the basis of their sexual ties and created a social world on the basis of a shared and marginalized community.... In such closets [as the gay baths] a gay world was built." (George Chauncey) As long as the homosexual was a reprobate, homos tended to (and had to) meet among themselves, for love encounters, as well as for solidarity, recognition, and protection. In the 1930s, a gay said: "All my life I have had to wear a rigid mask, a stiff armour of protection." Avoiding straights who are judgmental or aggressive and looking for the company of "people of my own type" forced homosexuals to lie and dissemble, to live a double life, particularly at work, often in the family as well. This went with a search for legitimacy via high culture (Greek love) or prestigious figures, often bisexual and worlds apart from the reality of modern times homosexuals, "exceptionally talented people like Socrates, Leonardo da Vinci, Michelangelo, Shakespeare, and Tchaikovsky," as Harry Whyte wrote to Stalin in 1934, not forgetting martyrs like Oscar Wilde, or more recently Alan Turing. Those references fortified a collective self-definition that gave the illusion of a community, as Foucault theorized it:

> The notion of mode of life seems important to me. Would it not be necessary to introduce a diversification other than that which is due to the social classes, to the differences of profession, to the cultural levels, a diversification that would be also a form of relation, and which would be the "mode of life"? A way of life can be shared between people of different age, status and social activity.... To be "gay" ... is not to identify with the psychological traits and the visible masks of the homosexual but to try and define and develop a mode of life. (Interview in *Gai Pied* no. 25, 1981)

The hitch is that any mode of life depends on the kind of *work* one does and one's place on the social spectrum. What do the lives of a gay Oxford don and a gay Tesco cashier have in common? At the most, they will briefly meet if they happen to share the same tastes, sexual preferences, for example, but the encounter is unlikely to last long because of the income and culture gap.

Even supposing a special way of life had existed, what could remain of it when the marginalization of same-sex loving people is on the wane, when a growing proportion of them have a family life, when sexuality does not define them any more than other criteria, such as education, profession, political or religious commitment, or leisure choices? There are as many differences between two same-sex couples as there are between two straight couples. As we will see in the next chapter, the notion of "homosexual culture" reduces culture to reference points. What is mistakenly thought of as identity is so fragmented it lacks the homogeneity necessary to determine an existence. As for the stereotyped multi-partner gay, his emotional life is close to that of the hetero minority—men and women—who go clubbing every weekend and come home with a different partner every Saturday night.

An LGBT World

In spite of everything that divides the gay lecturer from the lesbian who sweeps the college floor, they have good reasons to believe that they share a common condition caused by discrimination. Hence the idea of belonging to a set of minorities (gays, lesbians, bisexuals, transgender people, and intersex people), of which LGBT organizations would be the expression and champion—even more so in contemporary capitalism, where subcultures openly sprout, flower, and pollinate.

The wide range of LGBT groups, some fully independent, some semiofficial, profess to be the voice and defender of "sex and gender minorities." In reality, sexual reforms, including same-sex marriage, now legal in the United States and in an increasing number of European countries (which does not mean it's easy and unanimously approved of), are usually granted without mass street mobilizations, by right-wing governments (in Britain) as well as by left-wing ones (in France). Once the goal is achieved, gay and lesbian action manifests itself only by sporadic or symbolic gestures. LGBT associations regard themselves as the driving force of an evolution of which they are an effect. Like other advocacy groups, they react to events rather than shape them. In that respect, they basically differ from labor institutions; without worker rank-and-file pressure, the bourgeois would not have granted shorter working hours, social and unemployment benefits, etc., however limited and vulnerable these "conquests" are. Capital/wage labor relations and confrontations structure modern society. Gender does not.

Fighting the boss—even in a reformist way, which is the case in most labor struggles—is *not* fighting for *equality* between wage earner and bourgeois, because the employee cannot become his/her employer's equal, unless he/she becomes a boss him/herself, which is rarely possible. On the contrary, gays and lesbians, as gays and lesbians, want to be treated on the same footing as straights, and quite legitimately so, which boils down to a demand for *sexual equality*, a request that present society can grant, up to a point.

LGBT groups are born out of a situation in which public, official, and legal assimilation is countered by a persistent popular opposition. This contradiction gives them a social function. Their spokespersons (and members) can even genuinely believe themselves to be social critics. In fact, though they often happen to be going against the current, they are swimming in the long-term trend of capitalist history.

Identity, from Single to Multiple

The wide, deep, and confused proletarian wave of the 1970s attempted to fuse together workplace confrontations with daily life struggles—and failed. In the following decades, because of the defeat of workers, it looked as if the working class was no longer center stage, at least in Europe and the US, which is the part of the world we are writing about here, so there seemed to be no social fulcrum, no structural contradiction determining contemporary history.

While sexual minorities were being at least partially absorbed into society, and the bulk of the gay and lesbian movement went along with this evolution, a minority refused assimilation and turned to what they hoped were other potentially subversive groups.

In the halcyon days of the gay rebellion, the illusion that homosex practice is sufficient to bring *all* gays and lesbians together served as a rallying cry—for a while. Later, when the impetus had slowed down and melioration set in, some of the most militant elements grasped, to put it simply, the obvious gap between a gay bourgeois and a gay prole. So their belief in a sex-based commonality shifted into a search for multiple identities. Each group that faced discrimination would draw its strength from standing *on its own ground* and, at the same time, be able and willing to *associate with the others*. If sex was not enough of a salient mobilizing issue, a larger across-the-board coalition could be. In that sense, the gay and lesbian movement contributed to the rise of "identity politics."

Specific grievances, however, do not simply accumulate: each category usually pursues its own agenda. In fact, the greater the number of interlocked oppressed groups, the less they can achieve in common. Leslie Feinberg (1949–2014) described herself in 2006 as "an anti-racist white, working-class, secular Jewish, transgender, lesbian, female, revolutionary communist." In Leslie's *personal* political life, we can assume that these seven components blended fairly well. In *social groups*, however, quite a few members of each segment would refuse to associate with a lot people in each of the other six, so instead of a multiplying effect, the addition-subtraction process results in a coalition based on the lowest common denominator and can only set minimal goals. (Actually, such a collection is less numerous and cohesive than the supposedly outmoded working class.)

Not all gays have a joint interest in siding with other oppressed groups. For the gay civil servant persecuted on account of his homosexuality to make common cause with the precarious hetero worker, the railway engineer on strike, the laid-off shop-girl, the clandestine migrant, the battered wife, the beaten-up trans, and the jobless person victimized because of her skin color, it will take a social groundswell that moves him beyond the specificity of his sexual orientation—and to move each neighboring group beyond its own singularity. Otherwise, differences congregate without complementing each other.

Identity politics reflects social stratification rather than resisting or disentangling it.

War of the Words

Whereas the working class, by its sheer numbers, its insurrections, its pressure on the bourgeois, and its powerful reformist institutions hardly needed to prove its existence, contemporary allied and competing identity groups can only exist by gaining social and political visibility. Language is one of their major weapons; to be visible, one has to be called by one's appropriate name, hence an ongoing war of the words. "[T]he terminology problem—whether to use the word gay, lesbian, homosexual, homogenic, invert, sexual deviant, bisexual or something else entirely to describe the subjects of one's study—haunts the study of the history of sexuality." (Terence Kissack)

Indeed, quite a few readers must have raised an eyebrow at our writing on "homosexuals" (often shortened to "homos"), instead of "gays" and "lesbians." One of the reasons is that we prefer avoiding as much as possible the word "gay" at times when it would be anachronistic. Besides, if we are to refrain from talking about "homosexuals" because it is reductive, clinical, or simply too sexual, then logically we should also keep away from the term "hetero."

How did the word "gay" gain wide currency?

Charles Thorp, head of the gay group at San Francisco State College, declared in 1970:

Those who say they like the word Homosexual better than Gay say in essence that they accept our sick-psy-chiatrist friends' definition of us…. Homosexual is a straight concept of us as sexual. Therefore, we are in a sexual category and become a sexual minority … rather than an ethnic group, a people! But the word Gay has come to mean (by street usage) a life style in which we are not just sex machines…. We are whole entities…. Gay is a life style. It is how we live. (quoted by Neil Miller)

Fine, but for the "straight" as well, his/her love relation-ships are about a lot more than having sex. Homosexuality does not open up a totally different way of life than a hetero one, and why should it? When same-sex couples raise a child, travel, attend a political meeting, drive to the shopping center or to church, there is no reason why they would act differently than straight couples engaged in similar activities. There are as many ways of being straight as there are of being gay or lesbian, and the idea that gays could be "an ethnic group, a people" is just a pleasant fantasy.

The same writers and activists who object to the word "homosexual" are keen on theorizing homo-sociability and homoeroticism (as early as 1985 in Eve Kososfsky Sedgwick's *Between Men: English Literature and Male Homosocial Desire*). Commenting upon the film *Batman Forever* (1995), Raymond Murray spoke of a "dialogue that drips with homo-references." Probing into the *homoerotic* side of (non-gay) male writers has become a favorite research theme for scholars.

"Homo" is deemed acceptable in *homophobic* and objec-tionable in *homosexual*. Therefore, in *homosexual*, it is not the *homo* prefix people mind, it is the reference to *sex*, as if being gay, lesbian, bi, hetero, whatever had nothing or little to do with carnal attraction and physical desire, as well as pleasure. As if human emancipation could put aside our body and senses.

So this reluctance to speak of sex also dismisses "same sex." Are we to believe that abolishing the word "sex" helps to do away with sexism, homophobia, lesbophobia, transphobia, interphobia, genderphobia, glottophobia, LGBTphobia, whorephobia, etc.? Those who believe that a neutered language (and society) is the real way to nondiscrimination should hope for a human species of hermaphrodites.

Or is this de-sexing, this language cleansing, another lamentable example of sexphobia? The issue has been "sexed up," the discourse "sexed down," and the senses anesthetized. Euphemizing impoverishes and depletes speech and thought. Some past social reformers were less word-shy. John William Lloyd (1867–1940), author of poems on the vagina and penis, wrote that if the body is "reckoned obscene," then "life reeks" and "love rots."

It is unfortunate that "homophile" should sound outdated these days. As it denotes the fact that somebody loves people of the same sex, "homophile" has the merit of encompassing gays *and* lesbians, while "gay" only applies to men. "Homophile" should please those who care about inclusiveness. Regrettably, "homophile" is tinged with the idea of a half-assumed relation, with no commitment to action: platonic in other words. "Homosexual" is deemed inappropriate, because it emphasizes sex, "homophile" because it disembodies us; the former says too much, the latter too little. On the contrary, the superiority of the word "gay," and the reason for its worldwide success, is its ability to name a reality without saying anything concrete about it, while associating gay people with the positive image of a sunny disposition and a zest for festive life, as opposed to the supposed dreariness of straights. Who can resist the appeal of gaiety?

Language is never neutral. Whatever the remote origins of the word, the generalization of the term "gay" came with the development of the homosexual defense movement in the 1970s: calling themselves "gay" was a way for people to come out of the closet and publicly assert themselves against scornful and insulting epithets. It broke with prevailing representations: when homosexuals were alluded to in mainstream culture, they were either portrayed as perverted, ridiculous, or miserable characters. Reversing the roles, it is now the hetero who is caricatured as dismally constricted. A very old word was reborn as a milestone and a springboard. Later, with time, the militant word "gay" entered common media and political usage and became a blanket word for all those whose sexual orientation gives them a particular "identity." Painting in colors to avoid grayness.... We would rather hope that true emancipation will go for a "gaiety" shared by all walks of life and love.

Mario Mieli wrote in 1977 that *homosexual* is irrelevant as a substantive and should only be used as an adjective: one *is* not a homo. However, as he had to admit, our time cannot refrain from substantivizing, and the homo/hetero divide continues to reduce the scope of a potentially polymorphic sexuality.

Of course, words matter, but they do not come first. A social movement's vocabulary results from its grassroots activity. In its heyday, the labor movement would write and publish a lot, but the working class was strong enough to do without pamphlets specialized in the indispensable "class" wording. Nowadays, in many countries (Brazil, for example), LGBT groups circulate lexicons giving the appropriate word-list relating to gender—and updating them, needless to say.

Word obsession is a sign of half-failure, a proof of persisting limitation, an unavoidable one, for the moment. "Gay" has become a household word that serves both as a stepping-stone and a stumbling block. Coded—now mainstream—words like *gay* and *straight* "will be needed as long as there is a submerged and semi-legal society of homosexuals, and new words to meet new contingencies will have to be found." (Neil Miller)

CHAPTER 9

Gender and Genre: The Paradox of Gay Culture?

A Closeted Lesbian and Her Doubles: Patricia Highsmith

"Perversion interests me most and is my guiding darkness." (September 17, 1942)

"Am I a psychopath? Yes, but why not?" (January 7, 1943)

"Whatever pity I have for the human race is a pity for the mentally deranged and for the criminals.... Normal people bore me." (April 22, 1954)

"My personal *maladie* and malaises are only those of my own generation = of my time, heightened." (October 9, 1950)

"What keeps recurring to me as a fundamental of the novel is the individual out of place in this century." (September 25, 1952)

"My obsession with duality saves me from a great many other obsessions." (October 5, 1948)

These entries in the diary of Patricia Highsmith (1921–1995) could have been written by many twentieth-century Americans or European authors. Torn reality and split self are recurring themes of modern art. She was not the only one who wished in 1950 to "gather all the chaos of the world today and of my own soul and shape it into a story!" Nor was she an exception as a lesbian who wrote herself into her fiction. What is special in her novels is that they suggest a repressed sexual orientation by gender displacement: the woman-woman love that the writer could not or would not represent is narrated as if happening between men, except in the only book where the author—partially—removed the mask.

Though shelved as "crime," her novels are neither action-packed nor based on investigation. Detectives are more extras than leading characters in a plot that they have little control over. The identity of the criminal is a minor concern, and the novelist sometimes interchanged the victim and the culprit before completing the book. She focused on the relation between them: if one is murdered by the other, the other could just as easily have killed him. In her first novel, *Strangers on a Train* (1950), two men literally swap murders.

Her favorite character, Tom Ripley, appears in five novels. He never has sex with men, but what triggers the first murder, which will determine most of Tom's life, is his trying on his male friend Dicky's clothes and being caught at pretending to be Dickie in front of a mirror. Putting on someone's clothes is the nearest you can be to his body without touching him. Tom has an amazing gift for impersonation, dressing-up, and cross-dressing. This was decades before gender and transgendering became topical issues. "How grateful I am at last not ... to spoil my best thematic material by transposing it to false male-female relationships." (December 10, 1949)

She persisted in transposing lesbian love into an ambiguous relationship between two men. They meet, and one of them both befriends and dislikes the other, who is both dominated and charmed by the former. Each is attracted to the other, eventually kills him or wants to kill him, and crime there will be, but not necessarily between them; what matters is not who dies or the inquiry, let alone a social sanction (often the murderer gets away with it), only the ambivalence of what is in fact a couple relationship. In the words of one of her biographers, "She is the most unconsciously 'gay male novelist' since Ernest Hemingway." (Joan Schenkar)

Paying the Price of Salt

In 1948, while she was working in the toy section of a Manhattan department store, Patricia Highsmith briefly met a "blondish woman in a fur coat," who she helped to choose and order a doll for a child, and she took down the lady's address. As she recalled later, "I felt odd and swimmy in the head, near to fainting, yet at the same time uplifted, as if I had seen a vision." Back home, she wrote eight pages that summed up what was to be *The Price of Salt*: "It flowed from my pen as if from nowhere." A five-minute encounter with a woman (Kathleen Senn in real life) she never saw again was the starting point of a fiction, the only one of her novels without a violent death, also the only one with (moderately explicit) sexual scenes.

Patricia Highsmith imagined that the young shop assistant (named Therese in her fiction) and the customer (named Carol) meet again and engage in an intense friendship and love relation. Carol, however, is in the process of a divorce, and her "immoral" conduct (this is late 1940s) is used in court by her husband to apply for custody of their daughter. Carol has to choose between her child and her lover; she chooses Therese.

Patricia Highsmith knew her sexuality was an open secret in the intellectual and publishing world: "I suppose it's all over town. I am called a dyke." (November 24, 1950) However, she felt "shame for what [she had] done." Until 1989, she refused to allow *The Price of Salt* should appear under her name. Her explanation—or justification—was that she did not want to "be labelled a lesbian–book writer." In 1952, the novel was well received by critics, and it sold nearly a million copies a year later as a "pulp fiction" paperback, both a popular best-seller and a "cult" book in lesbian circles.

> The appeal of *The Price of Salt* was that it had a happy ending for its two main characters, or at least they

were going to try to have a future together. Prior to this book, homosexuals, male and female, in American novels had had to pay for their deviation by cutting their wrists, drowning themselves in a swimming pool, or by switching to heterosexuality ..., or by collapsing." (her 1989 afterword)

When Patricia Highsmith finally told the origin of the story, it was no "coming out." She was the opposite of a gay, lesbian, or sex rights fighter. Numerous testimonies and eight thousand pages of diaries and notes reveal an "extremely hostile and misanthropic personality." According to Andrew Wilson, her first biographer, she disliked most people and did not like herself much. "Miss Highsmith is an excellent hater," an English literary critic said in 1974. She was too self-centered to take a stand for homosexuality and was over-conscious of her inner troubled world, which she did not wish to directly turn into fiction. She did not want "peace of mind," she wrote in a 1947 "New Year's Toast": "I prefer to live with my neuroses and try to make the best of them." (1956 entry)

The Carol-Therese relation was too fulfilling and harmonious, too much of what Therese calls "a miracle," to be lived for real. The day the first draft of *The Price of Salt* was completed, Patricia Highsmith decided to take a look at Kathleen Senn's house (she had kept the address), and she went again six months later but never made contact: "Alas, should I see her, my book would be spoilt! I should be inhibited!" (June 5, 1950) She died without knowing that Kathleen Senn, an active but depressed woman, killed herself in 1951.

Ten years later, she planned another novel (prospectively titled *The Inhuman Ones*), "about the types of female homosexuals who have something missing from their hearts, who really hate their own sex" (December 1, 1961) but never got around to finishing it. Her last novel, *Small g: A Summer Idyll*, can be read as a book of reconciliation: straights, gays, and bisexuals meet and connect in free emotional flow. The nearest Patricia Highsmith could get to an agreement with herself... published posthumously.

Pulp to Mainstream

A novelist who wrote "Art is not always healthy, and why should it be?" (May 20, 1990) can hardly expect a good reputation. However, she has acquired respectability of late.

In the 1950s, *The Price of Salt* was published as "lesbian pulp," a subgenre of pulp fiction alongside western, gangster, etc.—cheap paperbacks, appreciated within a semi-clandestine lesbian subculture, because it was the only sort of book, Kate Millett said, where you could read about a woman kissing another woman.

On the screen as well, same-sex love was only present in the subtext, and actors' or directors' unconventional sexuality went unmentioned, Garbo's, Louise Brooks's, Dietrich's, James Dean's, and Marlon Brando's bisexuality, for example, or George Cukor's gay life. Farley Granger (one of the two main characters in Hitchcock's 1951 *Strangers on a Train*) was only open about his attraction to men when interviewed in the documentary *The Celluloid Closet* (1995).

Six decades after *The Price of Salt* was first published, this literary outcast of a book inspired a mainstream film titled *Carol*, a much less evocative title, which won critical acclaim and drew in millions of viewers. Homosexuality is no longer transgressive—on the screen anyway.

We've come a long way.

Have we? Same-sex women's love makes a "great" film, but life is not made of films. On the screen, people accept that the price to be paid for love is renouncing one's child, which was socially unacceptable in 1952, and remains so in 2022.

Patricia Highsmith was torn between a visible public life and what she felt was her censored deep self: "I am a walking perpetual example of ... a boy in a girl's body". (July 22, 1950)

Two years before, she had asked herself: "I want to change my sex. Is it possible?" (February 28, 1948)

A Problematic Definition

As proved by Patricia Highsmith's case, until recently, Western culture forced sexual minorities to take refuge in separate mental places and spaces, *sub*cultures in both senses, underground as well as disreputable. In response, to avoid being forced into self-denial, gays and lesbians had to go through a phase of personal *and collective* resistance. In Russia, after the publication of *Wings* (by Michael Kuzmin, in 1906, reportedly the first Russian novel to openly take homosexuality as its main theme), the poet Nikolaï Gumilev spoke in 1912 of "a whole array of people united by a common culture." (Dan Healey) Paradoxically, at the end of the twentieth century, this identity affirmation resulted in a new partitioning… granted, a self-imposed one.

It is not uncommon to hear people regret that the notion of a gay author is not widely acknowledged in France, whereas in the US many bookshops will have a "gay fiction" section. Edmund White wrote: "Perhaps the most telling contrast between France and the English-speaking world … is over the whole question of gay and lesbian literature."

What is meant by "gay author"? Is it a writer who is gay in his life? Or is it one who chooses gay characters and themes? Or is it both: a writer who is gay in his life and in his works? Or a writer that a "gay community" (defined how and by whom?) regards as one of their own? How much gay does one have to be to qualify as gay? No problem with Rimbaud, but what are we to do with the bisexual Verlaine? A lot of works by gays have nothing strikingly gay about them, while some works by straights deal with homosexual themes, so it is impossible to pinpoint where gayness begins and ends. "Gay themes" and "gay sensitivity" are areas either too narrow or too wide to warrant any valid demarcation.

It was highly positive that the artistic world could now reflect the possibility for gays and lesbians to present themselves as what they truly are and openly affirm what had long been a matter of secrecy, public shame, and disgrace. But why should this become an all-embracing definition of oneself, at the expense of all the other components of one's personality?

Defining somebody—a novelist or a plumber—on the basis of his/her sexual inclination downsizes him or her to a fraction of him/herself, as important as this part may be. Applied to artists, this criterion mutilates their production as much as their personality. True, we cannot understand Oscar Wilde and Jean Genet if we ignore their homosexuality, but it was not *the* essential, the element that determined all the rest. The richer and the more multifaceted an individual is, the less relevant it becomes to interpret him/her merely on the basis of his/her sexual dimension. James Baldwin wrote *Giovanni's Room* (1956) and numerous political essays in support of civil rights: What shelf is most adequate for him, "gay fiction" or "black studies"? James Whale made no secret of being gay: Is his best-known film *Frankenstein* (1931) gay? Authors who only partially deal with same-sex themes pose intractable problems: Balzac's *The Girl with the Golden Eyes* (1835) describes lesbian love: Should we detach this novella from the rest of his works and put it in "gay and lesbian fiction"? The undeniably heteronormative culture we live in does not prove the existence of a homogeneous gay and lesbian culture that would partake of an identity, unless we are content with a minimal identity deprived of everything unrelated to sex.

The writings that contribute the most to sexual emancipation express *more* than sexuality. Going back to *Giovanni's Room* in 1984, James Baldwin commented: "It's about what happens to you if you're afraid to lose anybody." Only a one-dimensional and depleted literature would be worthy of the "gay" label: books written by gays, for gays, telling gay stories. Something akin to genre books, manufactured to be shelved and easily found in specialized sections: "crime," "fantasy," "true stories," "romance," etc. What's worse, something easily prone to preaching and moralizing. Though he was overstating his case, Wilde had a point when he wrote from his cell in 1897 that "all bad art is the result of good intentions." This, of course, will always remain unacceptable to readers who expect a closed predictable ending and reject open ambiguity.

The addition of the "gay fiction" section in bookstores certainly signals growing public recognition, but this codification also maintains gays and lesbians in a separate category, as if their sexuality, though more and more accepted, continues to define them and set them apart. The closet has glassed-in doors now; it's a showcase. And "gay culture" only concerns a minority—the most visible, usually urban and moderately affluent—of all those who have same-sex practices.

By the way, if we suppose that there is enough in common—viewpoint, psyche, frame of mind, ethos—between gays for them to write specific fiction, i.e., novels or plays intrinsically different from those by heteros, then the same mental makeup is enough for them to write equally specific *nonfiction*. Logically, Foucault's books should not be located in the "philosophy" section but under "gay philosophy."

Borders do not protect; they fence us in.

Gore Vidal, historian, playwright, and novelist (author of *Myra Breckinridge*, 1968), refused to call himself a "gay writer": "to be categorized is, simply, to be enslaved," he commented, and anyway "I've said—a thousand times?—that everyone is bisexual."

"And Then We Quietly Fucked and Then We Slept"

The time is the 1850s, the place the United States, Thomas McNulty the narrator. When the story begins, he is a teenager, an Irish immigrant who has come to the US to escape poverty and death (his family died during the Great Famine). He meets John Cole. They become close friends and earn a living as cross-dressing entertainers in a town where there are no women. Despite padded breasts and makeup, the miners know they are dancing with boys. Just dancing: no sex. As they grow older, Thomas and John can no longer be "prairie fairies." They enlist in the army, fight in the Indian Wars and the Civil War, and are involved in their share of massacres. After the war, they become farmers in Tennessee, with black and white friends, get into trouble with Southern racists, risk their lives again...

This is a short summary of *Days without End*, a novel by Sebastian Barry (2016): let's leave the rest for readers to discover themselves.

The relationship between Thomas and John is loving and intimate. In the middle of the book, Sebastian Barry writes: "And then we quietly fucked and then we slept." No more about sex than this one-sentence nine-word paragraph. Genderwise, Thomas is "feminine" in his motherly caring of an adopted Indian girl and fondness for dressing in woman's clothes— and "masculine" in other respects, notably his soldiering.

"Gay fiction"? Sebastian Barry (born in 1955), playwright and novelist, is not known as gay; his main theme is more Ireland than sex, and *Days without End* belongs to a series of novels on the McNulty family across several locations and timeframes.

All we know is that one of his three children is gay, and that Toby coming out was important to the writing of the book, which bears the dedication "For my son Toby."

Days without End, however, explores the complexity and ambiguities of what is now called gender, the narration all the stronger since the novel never tries to make a point. (Incidentally, during the Civil War, Union army doctors reported four hundred women masquerading as men, only revealed as women when ill or wounded: it is likely there were many more.)

"And why worry about defining everything?" asked Therese in 1952.

CHAPTER 10

Being Gay or Lesbian in the Workplace

In the Steel Mill: An Invisible Class

Gary Works, in Indiana, used to be the biggest steel mill in the world and the flagship of the US Steel Corporation. Like the whole US steel industry, it keeps downsizing its labor force and Gary's population has declined from 170,000 in 1960 to 80,000 now. The Gary Works workforce dropped from 30,000 in the early 1970s to 5,000 in 2015 (out of which only 2,000 are now United Steel Workers members). Local people often think all steel production has ceased in the area. Steel being "central to the mythology of America" (Anne Balay), "working class people are reviled, often by themselves, so contempt is part of the work culture, easily applied to gay people," so the collapse of the steel industry "became a metaphor not only for decline and decay, but also for the loss of manhood." (Fonow, 2003) Actually, the prevailing image of the American worker as a white male remains statistically accurate: only 1 percent of the steel workforce is female, and there are very few blacks, even in Gary Works, although 85 percent of the town's population is black.

Anne Balay defines herself as a lesbian, LGBT activist, and "middle-class researcher," but she also worked for six years as a garage mechanic and, at one time, drove a heavy goods vehicle. In 2010–2011, she interviewed forty homosexuals employed in Gary Works: twenty men (one black), twenty women (two blacks, three Hispanics, one Asian), aged nineteen to sixty. The interviewees mostly described themselves as "gay," lesbians calling themselves "gay women." In income terms, they belong to the "upper" part of the working class, usually earning $60,000 to $100,000 per year... with lots of overtime, occupational accidents, and work-related diseases (unless stated otherwise, all subsequent related quotes are from Anne Balay).

"As gay people's visibility and acceptance have grown, the visibility and status of the mill workers have shrunk."

Masculinity, Male and Female

> The mill produces masculinity just as it produces steel, and anyone who fits in there both receives and generates that message ... self-presentation tends to be reactive ... motivated by change or opposition.... Masculine is one of those terms that resist definition except by recourse to their opposite. To be masculine is to be whatever your time and place defines as not feminine.

This is central enough for Anne Ballay to title her fourth chapter "Female Masculinity in the Steel Mill" and the subsequent one "Male Masculinity in the Steel Mill." She has a section titled "The Pleasure of Butchness."

Paradoxically, "for some gay women I interviewed, working in the steel mill provides an opportunity to give full expression to their masculinity, and get paid for it rather than punished." This confirms Anne's own experience as a mechanic in a male work environment. Biology is a secondary matter here: being a man is *acting like* a man. Some woman workers can be regarded as just as manly as men. "Though not all women in uniform are lesbians, they all benefit to some extent from the masculinity attributed to lesbians.... In both appearances and mannerisms, then, all female steelworkers might be thought of as honorary lesbians."

Wanda, tie-wearing and "very masculine," said: "at the mill I feel like it's my family." She is more at ease in the male-dominated mill environment than in the union where her female colleagues tend to be judgmental. In single-sex woman circles, the (relative) acceptance of what she is diminishes. On the street, a woman dressed like a man looks more like a cross-dresser and draws the gaze.

Therefore, in a way, it may be easier for a lesbian to work in a factory than in the service sector: "working class women are part of an aggressive culture where sexual banter passes time and physical contact is not anathema." Easier… providing she is able to out-tough men. This comes at a price.

Woman factory workers, heteros or not, are caught in a contradiction: they must display masculinity while remaining women. Whether straight or not, females disturb the male world: they cannot serenely read or watch porn ("pervasive" in conversations, lunch breaks, etc.) or laugh at inevitably sexist dirty jokes. They never quite fit in. Hence the possibility of aggression. The mill is far from a lesbian haven or even a safe place. The most extreme aggression reported in Gary Works targeted a transgender person.

Horseplayers and Regulars

Showers are the scene of "male camaraderie" that "in other contexts, would be taken for homoeroticism." Nate (about sixty) tells about a lot of penis-watching and/or -touching and physical contact. For Andy (in his thirties), "it is rare for a week to go by without some sort of sex at work" with married straight men. Fred has "a regular," and he used to have two. Transferred to a new department, he is asked by a fellow-worker: "Is it true you're gay? I said yeah, he said 'Want to suck my dick?' … [I]n my old department we called this guy number 7 because he was going to be my seventh."

If this is "having sex," it certainly is not "homosexuality": "guys get very explicit… as long as you're not gay." (Nate) Anne Balay comments: "Male-male sex is public, something you do at work, while male-female sex is private, stays at home, and is what counts. Though this constitutes a divide between the public and the private, it's not the divide we're used to, in which all sex stays home."

Similarly, an Australian survey revealed "a continuum of homoerotic experience among working class men ... [but] the experience is silenced [and] the public language of the peer group is heterosexual. Moreover, it is seriously homophobic."

Wanda, black, butch, and "masculine-looking," was aggressively hassled by men who had trouble situating her: Was she "male" or "female"? In 1967, Elise first worked in the mill as a man: when she came back a woman in 1994, her workmates were so violently hateful that the management had a security guard protect her. Horseplay is fun, even a blow job can be fine (within limits), but openly transgressing binary norms is repulsive.

Invisible Gays and Lesbians

No male worker calling himself "normal" (straight) would hint at the homosexual acts that take place in the mill (and outside: sometimes male same-sex practices go on at home, when the wife and kids are away). A number of them are participants, and many others know about it, but if the subject happens to be broached, they are "horrified," and logically so, because such behavior could have them perceived as *gay*, which very few of them would be able to accept.

"The mill is an environment in which men can give and receive oral sex without seeing themselves as queer." In 2001, Kitty Krupat wrote: "homophobia is ... a unifying issue. In a workplace, homophobia can be the one thing many people agree on." A gay left Gary Works because of harassment and hostility and got a job with the police; it is sad "that New York police force would provide more acceptance of gay employees than a steel mill." All Anne Balay's interviewees' names are aliases. She had to be very discreet when meeting them, and she received death threats while preparing her survey.

Gay and lesbian Gary Works employees live a double life (straight workers too, as the sex they have at work is unmentionable at home, but they do not suffer harassment because of it). They are also isolated: most interviewed people thought they were the only gay in basic steel.

Alice Puerala (1928–1986), labor and civil rights activist, was the first woman elected at the head of the United Steelworkers (USW) local in 1979: with workmates and union comrades, she kept quiet about her bisexuality. Neighborhood people would deny she was a lesbian, although they were aware of her living with another woman. In fact, she was initially more open about it, then "it became a kind of quiet thing" as she moved up in the USW hierarchy and acquired a public image. Does the currently expanding geography of gay and lesbian freedom stop at the factory gates?

Work Community

> Working in a steel mill is a lot like being in combat. The danger and isolation of the job create a bond between co-workers … the danger of the work creates a camaraderie…. Social interaction and community building are important parts of mill culture.

As seen in chapter 8, from the 1970s onward, to defend themselves, gays (i.e., a number of them large enough to act as a social force) formed a community (no more imaginary than many others) disconnected from work and, therefore, a trans-classist community. Gary Works is rather the opposite: to collectively face the management, the workers' group exists on the assumption of a shared heterosexuality. When same-sex love does happen in the mill, probably more than among teachers on school premises, it is not sex, it is play. In the steel mill, class is male: women are far better integrated if they act like men. In Gary Works, class is hetero. Even a lesbian union official like Alice had to wear a heterosexual mask.

> For steel workers, one component of community is their unions…. Yet [gay and lesbian] communities work only because they're isolated from work and family, allowing members to remain invisible except to each other … the separation of sexual identity from work life that characterizes queer sociability makes it difficult for unions to identify and protect their LGBT members, even if they wanted to.

Including Canada and the Caribbean, the USW boasts about 1.2 million members and is the largest union in the US private sector. At the time of Anne Balay's study (2010–2011), none of the hundreds of people who work in its headquarters openly declared themselves to be gay or lesbian.

Work creates an experience of *us* vs. *them*, and what defines this *us* cannot be impervious to what prevails in society at large: sexism, for example. The high proportion of woman factory workers has little effect on this phenomenon as long as work remains sex-segregated: most men and women do not do the same jobs. Today's "feminization of trades" is partly an optical illusion and is more tangible in the service sector. Few women work on building sites, and fewer still are heavy equipment operators.

Capitalism did not invent sexism, but it uses it—just as it uses racism—to reinforce divisions between proletarians. To defend themselves, the workers' *we* line up against the bosses' *them*, but not infrequently this *we* also makes common cause against real or supposed competitors on the labor market. In that event, the *we* bloc can then be based on a specific trade, region, nation, sex, color, or any combination of the above, against women, foreigners, blacks, etc., anyone likely to be or be presented as a scab or likely to "steal our jobs." Of course, gays and lesbians are not going to take jobs away from the straights, but the more cohesive and closed-in the worker community remains, the more protective it is or is believed to be.

If being a steel worker no longer guarantees masculinity since layoffs, give-backs, corporate takeovers and negative media attention all collude to make even steelworkers with jobs feel insecure and defensive, then steelworker masculinity must be reinforced through the exclusion of women and gay men.

The trouble with identity is that there is always more than one, so identity clashes are inevitable. This poses the thorny question of how the proletarians can overcome divisions among themselves. As Anton Pannekoek said, "The working class is not weak because it is divided; on the contrary, it is divided because it is weak." How can the proletarians cease to be weak? As there will never be jobs for everyone (at best, there will be temp, precarious, and low-paid employment for most people), a community made up only of those at work can only unite part of the proletarians, who are indifferent or hostile to other parts; some will achieve solidarity at the expense of others. Wage laborers will only get beyond their divisions by getting rid of wage labor. But that's another story, which remains to be lived and told.

Masculine Image Still Sets the Rules

Fabrice, a French factory worker in his thirties, is gay. Where he works, he has neither experienced anything similar to the male sex play going on in Gary Works nor heard of gay harassing or bashing—possibly because he is committed to interim work, mostly on building sites, and when installing or repairing machines in a factory he never stays more than a few months. Very unlike the community life familiar to Gary steel workers.

I started working in 2003, but the first time I told a work mate that I often had sexual relations with men was 2009, eight years ago. For a long time, my sexuality did not exist, it was unimaginable to mention it at work. When you meet work colleagues, pretty soon they ask you about your family, your kids, your wife. For a long time I would say "Well, no, I'm single." This kind of schizophrenia drove me crazy! I just can't anymore… when the question is raised I don't evade the issue.

Asked if it is because the times have changed, Fabrice replies he has not seen "any deep societal changes on the matter" since the early 2000s: it is he who has become more self-confident. When he now replies, "I have a boyfriend" or "I often have boyfriends," people at work are usually surprised or respond "that's OK" or "nothing wrong with that." So far, he has never gotten into trouble because of "that," but he realizes that what kept him silent for years was the dominant male sociability; when people engage in small talk and have a laugh, the "implicit general thing is that gays are disgusting. There are plenty of gross jokes about gays."

But maybe there is something else to it, and what I have heard from other people rather confirms it: I look like a man, a worker as usually portrayed, I speak with a deep voice, I neither dye my hair pink nor polish my nails. I wonder what would happen if that was not the case, if I gave free rein to my feminine side. It is certainly more difficult to assert a certain femininity at work than to say that when you go home you will fuck a man. I had a trans friend, an electrician working quite normally in the building trade: the day people saw on his ID a woman's name, it became absolute misery, jokes, persecution day after day, until he could not take it anymore. It was not strictly sexuality that mattered, it was this femininity/masculinity question. Judging from the feedback I get from guys working in typically masculine jobs, it's the same nightmare everywhere. It seems to be easier for those in predominantly female jobs (nursing, care, or retail trade) to live their sexuality or part of their femininity. Whereas, in all the workplaces I've known, I never came across any guy mentioning his homosexuality.... So, on the one hand, affirming my sexuality at work has appeared to me a lot simpler than I had been fearing for years. But, on the other hand, that fear, that social pressure, I am not the only one to experience it. Otherwise, why would so many guys remain in the closet? As far as sexuality goes, in my jobs, I have the impression it's the anxiety that is the most repressive, a lot more than "repression" properly speaking.

Regarding femininity, I feel it's a different kettle of fish.... A lot of people imagine that all gays more or less fit in with a certain stereotype, and that they're a bit effeminate. And perhaps that's what really disturbs them the most.

CHAPTER 11

Queer, or the Identity That Negates Identities

In the post-Stonewall period, a wing of the lesbian and gay movement was not content with just being socially accepted (or tolerated), was dissatisfied with the mere affirmation of a gay/lesbian "identity," and was angered by quarter measures that were obviously inadequate against the ravages of the HIV-AIDS epidemic. This militant minority reclaimed an old word that often had a pejorative connotation yet was also sometimes used by homosexuals themselves: *queer*.

Bad Girls

By the early 1960s, John Howard explains, "queer no longer denoted a nebulous eccentricity but was used as an epithet of sexual gender and racial non-conformity.... *Queer* [held] multiple meaning." For the Mississippi "queers," it was "an expansive definition that [went] well beyond homosexuality to encompass all thoughts and expressions of sexuality and gender that are non-normative or oppositional."

A couple of decades later, Dorothy Allison remembers:

> The Sex Wars are over, I've been told, and it always makes me want to ask who won. But my sense of humour may be a little obscure to women who have never felt threatened by the way most lesbians use and mean the words *pervert* and *queer*. I use the word queer to mean more than lesbian. Since I first used it in 1980 I have always meant it to imply that I am

not only a lesbian but a transgressive lesbian-femme, masochistic, as sexually aggressive as the women I seek out, and as pornographic in my imagination and sexual activities as the heterosexual hegemony has ever believed.... My sexual identity is intimately constructed by my class and regional background, and much of the hatred directed at my sexual preferences is class hatred—however much people, feminists in particular, like to pretend this is not a factor. The kind of woman I am attracted to is invariably the kind of woman who embarrasses respectably middle-class, politically aware lesbian feminists. My sexual ideal is butch, exhibitionistic, physically aggressive, smarter than she wants you to know, and proud of being called a pervert. Most often she is working class, with an aura of danger and an ironic sense of humour.

Pat (now Patrick) Califia, involved in support groups for S and M people, wrote in 1982: "The gay community has less and less tolerance for folks whose sexuality cannot be clearly defined as heterosexual or homosexual or who have erotized something other than gender." The following year, she added: "I live with my woman partner of five years. I have lots of casual sex with women. Once in a while I have casual sex with gay men. I have a three-year relationship with a homosexual man who doesn't use the word *gay*. And I call myself a lesbian." Though "I identify more strongly as a sadomasochist than as a lesbian ... most of my partners are women, but gender is not my boundary, I am limited by my own imagination."

To mention but a few rebels that would not submit: Off Our Backs (1970), The Furies (1971), COYOTE (1973, a prostitutes' organization), Combahee River Collective (1977), Samois (lesbian S and M group, 1978), and the Feminist Anticensorship Task Force (1984) were among the disruptors who reacted to the mainstream homosexual rejection of "deviants."

Dominant feminism had the high moral ground and closed ranks against "bad girls" like Lisa Duggan, who could hardly claim moral rectitude; her struggle against porn censorship—a censorship sponsored by a large proportion of feminist circles—was enough to give her a bad name. An excellent opportunity for exercises in slur and slander and, as the saying goes, "accusations are convictions in the public mind."

Though not world-famous like Judith Butler, Lisa Duggan happens to be one of the founders of the "queer" phenomenon. In 1991, she realized the limit of the "liberal" attempt to give gays and lesbians a minority status comparable to that of blacks and women, with rights equal to other citizens, but she also refused a "ghetto" that would primarily benefit privileged white lesbians and gays. Rather, she wished to build a "queer community" made up of all sexually marginalized people who try to live the circulation of their desires without restraint, fear, or culpability. (This went against the notion of the "by birth" gay who lives a condition he has not chosen.)

"We might begin to think about sexual difference, not in terms of naturalized identities, but as a form of *dissent*, understood not simply as speech, but as a constellation of nonconformist practices, expressions and beliefs." ("Queering the State," 1994)

Thus posited, queer suggests the possibility of an overall social (dis)solution. Consequently, if they do not insist in adhering to stereotypes, some heteros could be part of it: one is not a hetero queer or a homo queer; one is first and foremost a queer.

From then on, *queer* functioned in opposition to *gay*. Whether they admit it or not, those who call themselves gays put desire for same-sex love among the essentials of their lives. *Gay* is always an "identity-based description," whereas *queer* can be connected or disconnected from any specific description. In the 1990s, queer started to be applied to non–socially integrated sexual life; it called for a "coalition of the marginalized." (John Howard) Gay is identity; queer is beyond identities. It purports to fully "denaturalize" sex and promotes transitions and back-and-forth movement between "normality" and "deviance."

Queer Nation

What would have remained limited in scale soon mushroomed into a social movement because of the HIV-AIDS epidemic, notably the mobilization organized around Act Up. As we saw in chapter 7, Act Up did not just fight to improve treatment and care for patients, it also questioned the conformism of an increasingly institutionalized gay movement. Though a splinter group, the queers were a very active minority, who helped transform the attitude of American society faced with the AIDS crisis.

At the 1990 New York Gay Pride, some people marching with the ACT UP contingent handed out a *Queer Nation Manifesto* that proclaimed:

> Straight people are your enemy. They are your enemy when they don't acknowledge your invisibility and continue to live in and contribute to a culture that kills you.... An Army of Lovers Cannot Lose.... Being queer means leading a different sort of life.... It's about being on the margins.... And we are an army of lovers because it is we who know what love is. Desire and lust, too. We invented them.... We've given so much to that world: democracy, all the arts, the concepts of love, philosophy and the soul, to name just a few of the gifts from our ancient Greek Dykes, Fags.... Your life is in your hands....
>
> Why Queer? ... Well, yes, "gay" is great. It has its place. But when a lot of lesbians and gay men wake up in the morning we feel angry and disgusted, not gay. So

we've chosen to call ourselves queer. Using "queer" is a way of reminding us how we are perceived by the rest of the world. It's a way of telling ourselves we don't have to be witty and charming people who keep our lives discreet and marginalized in the straight world. We use queer as gay men loving lesbians and lesbians loving being queer. Queer, unlike *gay*, doesn't mean *male*.

Founded in 1990 as a group within Act Up, Queer Nation soon split to address broader issues beyond AIDS campaigns, as illustrated by one of its slogans: "We are everywhere; we want everything." Being queer is to oppose any discrimination, be it based on gender, race, or class. Queer Nation also refused to demand rights, which was the main concern of the organizations that started being labeled LGBT at the end of the 1980s.

The *Manifesto* did not give any definition of *queer* other than *acting as queer*, i.e., against all forms of exclusion and oppression. In lieu of an identity (gay, working-class, Afro-American, Latino, woman, etc.), queer represented a commitment in conflict with what was becoming mainstream homosexual politics, and fighting AIDS was only one queer objective among others. "Queer" put topical issues on such a wide canvass that it meant breaking away from the whole of society. No wonder its activity stayed on the fringe of a homosexual movement that insisted on calling itself "gay" or "lesbian," not "queer."

In the context of the 1980s, after two decades of social struggles that ended in defeat and the rise of neoliberalism, the equation "queer = deviant = discriminated-against = dominated = rebel" became a point of reference for those in pursuit of a general perspective going beyond sexual matters, but who could not or would not think in class terms. Those who called themselves "queer" were fully aware that heteronormative pressure did not bear in the same way on a business lawyer and his cleaning lady, but as class analysis, and even more so participation in a supposedly defunct class struggle, seemed utterly impossible, queer gave them a way of talking and dealing with social division while deemphasizing the exploitation of labor by capital. The general theme of domination came to center stage instead.

This implied working toward the convergence of every specific struggle, i.e., all communities getting together; "alliance" and "coalition" were key notions. However, what emerged was the opposition between those who combat domination and those who are accused of reveling in it. Queer activity contrasted norm-accepters and norm-refusers, so the enemy was the normed, the normative, and finally the hetero.

Revolution is *now* if we devote our energy to it, proclaimed Queer Nation, which pinned its hopes on retrieving the momentum lost since Stonewall.

In a time of declining struggles, the manifesto's call to arms could only cause disappointment. "Queer" was being forced to move onto different terrains.

Academic Queer

After 1993, *queer* lost most of its militancy at the same time as it reached out to a larger audience. It had its lifestyle, its mannerisms, its cinema, its shops, its travel agencies. At the very time Queer Nation was disappearing from nearly all US cities, academics like Lisa Duggan thought it possible to animate—or reanimate—it in lectures and symposiums. *Queer* became *queer theory*.

On both sides of the Atlantic, 1970s Marxist leftism only ever occupied the basements of intellectual life, hardly ever the upper floors. Queer theory was infinitely better adapted to a postmodernism made of the decomposed fragments of radical thought. People had had enough of general theories offering global historical views (the fact that such theories were labeled "grand narratives" testifies to the prevalence of linguistics and cultural studies: the prioritization of language will be dealt with below). Reality was broken down into multitudinous forms of power and degrees of hegemony, and collective action to transform reality was divided into a series of practices disconnected from class confrontation. Marxism was discarded for "essentialism" (*essence* being the postmodern code word for whatever intellectual heavy hitters of the day do not acknowledge).

Failing anything better, Queer Nation had used the word *queer* to bring together its various fields of struggle despite their blurred contours. Academics now theorized "queer" as separate spheres… and kept wondering how to reconnect each sphere with the others.

It did not really matter that nobody knew what "queer" was. It was enough that "queer" put groups side by side; the addition would transcend divisions. "Queer" believed that people of color, feminists, gays, lesbians, anti-globalizers, eco-activists, etc., would, together, create a political force able to turn the world upside down.

"Queer" was an ideological unifier that helped to avoid reflection on a double defeat: the failure of the 1970s "sexual revolution" to be the harbinger of social revolution and the demise of the gays and lesbians who regarded homosexuality as the ultimate subversive tool. "Queer" came at the right time. Unlike Marxism, it had the immense advantage of having no totalizing ambition; it gave preeminence to the diverse, the diffuse, the sectioned, the porous. A basic tenet of the "deconstruction" bombshell that rocked study halls and college dorms was the idea that society has no center of gravity, therefore no social force of gravity.

The role of the university queer was to broaden the field of gay and lesbian questions but only by depriving them of their initial radical surge. In the 1970s, social antagonisms had forced sociologists to take class into account. After 1980, when conflicts in the workplace weakened, when the factory workers sank from view, researchers and scholars modified their mental framework: exploitation gave way to domination, a concept that could encompass just about anything. At the end of the twentieth century, and not just on the Western side of the Atlantic, women's studies were diluted with gender studies and cultural studies, which were in turn "subsumed" under subaltern studies.

Queer became a verb in its own right: queering the state, queering theory, queering academia.... In 1991, Lisa Duggan believed in academic activism: a year later, her hopes were dashed at the Fifth Lesbian and Gay Studies Conference at Rutgers. University is the production line for intellectual elites and opinion shapers; you cannot expect it to subvert society. Radical critique only finds its way in PhDs and exam papers to have its teeth pulled out.

Death of the Subject

Judith Butler is not the inventor of "queer theory" (the word *queer* is absent from her *Trouble in Gender* [1990], regarded as a foundation stone). She owes her celebrity to her critique of a feminism that had reacted to masculine domination by valorizing a feminine identity. Instead of stressing what women have in common, Judith Butler suggested "a radical critique of identity categories." Feminism will run aground, she said, if it lets itself be boxed in any feminine definition, however positive. "Queer" is a refusal to be assigned to anything.

So far, so good. But *Trouble in Gender* did not simply challenge the "woman" category as a historical subject, it also dismissed any subject that would be the "ultimate candidate to representation, or indeed, liberation," because any chosen "political subject" or "stable subject" excludes others: for her, no social group is central to how society reproduces itself.

Queer theory looks for the way "the major systems of oppression" are "interlocking" without any *one* (certainly not wage labor) determining the others. Domination forms are intertwined, and their deconstruction could only result from a bloc of fighting categories, especially sex and gender minorities. The queer program advocated a coalition of socially excluded groups, and each single identity (female, for example) was to be completed by others. There is no unique or main historical agent: the agents are innumerable—literally—and counting them would be setting limits and would be next to oppressive. Only the infinite addition sets people free, and queer theory can tell a true emancipatory movement by its ability to always include yet one more minority.

Performing

Unlike Marx, who probed into the bourgeois/proletarian contradiction based on production relations, Judith Butler is interested in a repetition relation; in her eyes, repetition perpetuates submission and is bolstered by the way people behave, and particularly by language. Domination occurs because the dominated accept it via reiteration: the solution will come from interrupting the process, from breaking the repetition cycle. If present social life is made of behavior and discourse, other behavioral patterns will deconstruct it by "subversive bodily acts." If gender forces us to play roles that make us men or women, we will find a way out of it by changing from a single imposed role to various chosen ones.

Enter "performativity," a concept borrowed from linguistics. It designates sentences that just by being spoken carry out a certain action, like saying one's vows, making a promise, or a judge pronouncing a sentence. However, even in the linguistic field, the notion is only valid to a limited extent. Speech does not "perform" in the sense that on its own it can have an impact on reality. For marriage to be effective, the words "I declare you husband and wife" have to be uttered by special people in an institutional context, and then confirmed by an appropriate administrative procedure. The same applies to "we declare war." Language is never enough.

Judith Butler chooses to ignore this basic fact. For her, society is not based on the division between those who control the means of living and those who do not. It depends on who masters knowledge and language. As a logical conclusion, the political solution lies in resisting control via reappropriating language.

"Thanks to performatives, language becomes action," writes Paul B. Preciado. Believing that "Saying Is Doing" is indispensable to whoever wishes to give priority to speech, to "discursive formation," "the discursive effect," "discursive production," i.e., to word power, as eloquently said by the French title (*Le pouvoir des mots*) of Butler's *Excitable Speech: A Politics of the Performative* (1997). The social *is* the textual, or vice-versa.

Poets and novelists always have a tendency to overemphasize the "alchemy of the word" (Rimbaud), which is their source material and their natural habitat. Taking the word for the deed: nobody has expressed it better than a character in Saul Bellow's novel *Herzog* (1964): "I go after reality with language. Perhaps I'd like to change it all into language."

When transferred from art to history and turned into political theory, this proclivity is ideal for the teacher, the educator, the activist, or a possible mixture of all three. When—as in Foucault—social power mechanisms are reduced to discursive patterns, challenging the "hegemonic cultural discourse" and current "regimes of truth" is the key.

This theory has been well received because it seems to go beyond feminist and LGBT claims, and because it suggests activities that are both accessible and attractive; inoffensive transgression always has a strong appeal. Nineteen-seventies "consciousness-raising" has now been complemented by provocative innocuous gestures.

Moreover, "performativity" is convoluted enough to be immune to refutation. To perform is to play, to represent (as on a stage), but also to do, to accomplish, so the theorist can always argue that his/her performing is modifying reality by empowering him/her with agency, when, in fact, he/she is playing with codes and merely subverting forms of expression.

Citizen Queer

There is no revolutionary essence in queerness. It has its revolutionaries and its moderates, its street activists and its academic luminaries. The same theoretical framework can generate diverse and conflicting avatars. Bernstein, Lenin, and Rosa Luxemburg all availed themselves of the *class* concept, which they interpreted in different ways. On a much smaller scale, "queer" morphed into unexpected outgrowths, some radical like the one examined in the next paragraph, some deliberately aiming at reform.

Judith Butler has now expanded what she believed to be the creative power of language (except language for her is more than language; she equates it with action) to the democratic reunion of the oppressed; it's now whole crowds who will be performing. The "resistant subjectivity" of 1990 has moved from individual to assembled bodies, and creative speech is presented as globally transformative. The body is not just dissenting, it can form the body politic: people—i.e., probably the famous 99 percent—meet to debate, and collective debating is a first step on the road to changing the world.

In the past, *queer* was synonymous with grassroots self-organization; some proponents of queer theory now vindicate electoral democracy as a possible extension and complement of direct democracy. In the midst of the ongoing crisis of the "old-school" left, a new vision of the agora could not fail to resonate with attempts to renovate reformism. The "political performativity of assemblies" concept easily blends into the various Occupy "squares" and "citizens" movements.

It is no accident that the pragmatic wing of queerness should have crossed paths with efforts to build a refurbished left. Unlike former socialist parties, Spanish Podemos and Greek Syriza are not based on organized labor but on a gathering of social movements structured by local democracy, ecology, gender, and minority issues.

"How could we reconstitute a *people*?" That is the contemporary reformer's dilemma. Their answer is: not as an aggregate of millions of individuals or fractioned disordered groups, but a "demos," a collective body, diverse yet cohesive enough to implement reasonable social change. Late nineteenth- and twentieth-century bourgeois democracy worked on the basis of a confrontational meeting of capital and labor and a mixture of reform and conservatism. With organized labor on the wane, twenty-first century "integrative citizenship" hopes for an "inclusive" approach no longer based on class but on a combination of "societal" differences and demands grounded in sex, origin, race, color, environment problems, etc., the laboring world only being one actor among many.

"Moderate" queers could not fail to see the impossibility of politics founded on homosexuals as a whole (lesbians, gays, trans, etc., having no common interests apart from sex/gender issues). So they looked further and hoped to encourage all dominated groups to converge as "an assembled people." New *worldmaking* would be supported by sexual, as well as social, collective grassroots practices, micro-politics, and auto-experimentation that could build up enough solidarity to resist and then dismantle neoliberalism. Global revolution has been replaced by millions of local revolutions.

This new agora program is close to the "commons" theory, with special emphasis on the sex/gender question. It purports to reconcile bottom-up and top-down politics and to eventually lead to a reform-friendly government. At least, that's the plan... unrealistic in what remains a class society—a fundamental fact dismissed or denied by all variants of the queer spectrum that we know of.

Queer Extreme

The gay and lesbian movement initiated at the time of Stonewall only had a revolutionary character in the short historical span when it coincided with worldwide social storms; its program was subversive, because at that time established society denied and criminalized same-sex love. The (granted, relative and contradictory) integration that followed was only regarded as a defeat by a minority of activists; for most lesbians and gays, it was a victory to be able to become combat soldiers, company executives, or political leaders without having to hide what they were. From the closet to the rostrum: so far, five European heads of government have publicly come out before being elected: two lesbians and three gays, in Iceland (2009), Belgium (2011), Luxemburg (2013), then Ireland and Serbia (2017).

This insurrectionist queers know and will not admit: they are searching for the silver bullet that will explode the historical deadlock.

While a lot of far-left groups (ex-Trots, etc.) propose some peaceful way to social change, insurrectionist anarchism has the immense merit of insisting on insurrection as a sine qua non of revolution. It expounds an indispensable critique of the discourse of rights: "Assimilation is the master tool for the liberal ruling class. Assimilation is typically initiated by the discourse of rights." (Fray Baroque and Tegan Eanelli, *Queer Ultra Violence: Bash Back! Anthology* [2011]: unless stated otherwise, all subsequent related quotes are from this book.)

Basically, insurrectionist queers maintain that there can be no "sexual liberation" outside of social revolution, and that only "queer" opens the way for social revolution.

What is "queer"?

Queer is not merely another identity that can be tacked onto a list of neat social categories, nor the quantitative sum of our identities. Rather, it is the qualitative

position of opposition to presentations of stability—
an identity that problematizes the manageable limits
of identity. Queer is a territory of tension, defined
against the dominant narrative of white-hetero-mo-
nogamous-patriarchy, but also by an affinity with all
who are marginalized, otherized and oppressed. Queer
is the abnormal, the strange, the dangerous. Queer
involves our sexuality and our gender, but so much
more. It is our desire and fantasies and more still....
Queer is the cohesion of everything in conflict with
the heterosexual capitalist world.... By "queer," we
mean "social war."

To recap, "queer" bridges all gaps. A 2009 leaflet spoke
of all the dominated and oppressed, "trans, women, POC
[persons or people of color]," which means millions, billions,
certainly not defined by class, however:

When we speak of social war, we do so because purist
class analysis is not enough for us. What does a Marxist
economic worldview mean to a survivor of bashing? To
a sex worker? To a homeless, teenage runaway? How
can class analysis, alone as paradigm for a revolution,
promise liberation to those of us journeying beyond
our assigned genders and sexualities? The Proletariat
as revolutionary subject marginalizes all whose lives
don't fit in the model of heterosexual-worker.

Really? It is doubtful that a gay bourgeois and a gay prole
equally risk and suffer bashing, so class analysis is not as
irrelevant as it might seem.

More importantly, if "social war" is not determined by
"economic" working conditions, what causes it? We are told
that "queer" is what stands in out-and-out opposition to the
existing world, so society is to be criticized "from the point
of view of queer experience," which joins the experience of

all marginalized and oppressed people. Radical queer politics starts from what sexual minorities can have in common with people of color, transgender persons, migrants, sex workers, the poor, and the most deprived. In other words, categories of people who are not only the most oppressed but also do not oppress others: for instance, this excludes workers who engage in sexist or racist behavior and those middle-class gays and lesbians who despise transgenderism. So, not simply the "wretched of the Earth," but the *most* wretched.

The insurrectionist queer is looking for a substitute proletariat, one with more "radical chains" than the until now mainly reformist working class and believes it is found it in the lowest of the low, groups selected for their social and sexual unacceptability. Unfortunately, just as few factory workers take to the street to promote gay rights, not every homeless woman sides with sex workers, not all people of color support undocumented migrants, not all migrants care about abused women, etc. There is nothing universal *in itself* about the wage earner's fight against his boss or in the struggle of the sexual minority.

It is alleged that "entire populations" are about to join queer activity. Why would they? Because—and here we get to the core of queer theory—the need for freedom is smoldering under the embers, caused by the utmost oppression inflicted upon millions, like a long-repressed subversive potential waiting to be rekindled. By what? By the action of a queer minority able to force events? To hope for that, one has to believe in the virtue of exemplary action and in the efficiency of militant activism. Which is precisely what the insurrectionist queer believes in: the possibility that a minority can "create a strong queer counterculture that could challenge capitalism ... by building a culture of attack" fueled by desire mixed with anger: "Time and again non-violent detractors have raised questions regarding the validity of tactics rooted in anger. These dogmatic agents of control cannot grasp why the queer proletariat would be motivated to adopt a position of attack at any time and without hesitation."

Supposing the queer minority was strong enough to build up spaces that would allow for the unconstrained flow of desire, it is hard to imagine that they could at the same time remain antagonistic to existing society. Or, rather, it is logical to think they would, if you believe—as queer theory does—that desire is always a bearer of radicalism that no society can integrate or absorb. (The old workers' movement also thought its "counter-society" was immune to bourgeois pressures and capable of eventually disaggregating capitalism.)

The queer bottom line is a deep belief in the inherently subversive capacity of sex—a capacity queer theory thinks class exploitation does not provide. Sexuality is perceived as alien to order, rebellious by nature, and, therefore, bound to conflict with authority; it will just take the right spark to ignite the fuse that will blow up all oppressions.

The undermining potential of sex provides queerness with the ultimate historical leverage. (Give me a lever and the right place to stand, and I will move the earth, Archimedes reportedly said.) In the 1970s too, "Sex appeared as an uncontrollable force that spawned social chaos when its power was let loose." (John D'Emilio and Estelle Freedman) This allows any segregated and persecuted sexuality to be presented as a vector of subversion: homosexuality forty years ago, transgenderism today.

Let's go back to the questions: "What does a Marxist economic worldview mean to a survivor of bashing? To a sex worker? To a homeless teenage runaway?" It won't do just to turn the question round and ask: "What does gay bashing or the plight of sex workers mean to a laid-off factory operative?" The mistake is to look for the most downtrodden and, therefore, the most likely to revolt. Revolution is indeed the time when the exploited (factory or sex) worker and the oppressed sexual minority realize what they have in common and fight against it. But there's no magic recipe for that.

The Identity That Refuses to Be

Defining oneself as "queer" meant a dissatisfaction with the affirmation of gayness, lesbianism, or bisexuality and a demand for freedom and fluidity. Deviant bad girls, Queer Nation, academic queer, pragmatic queer, and ultraqueer could all endorse Fray Baroque and Tegan Eanelli's statement: "We view queer as the blurring of sexual and gender identities. Queer is the refusal of fixed identities." "Queer" was born as a dissidence against dominant sex forms: in reaction to the social integration of the LGBT galaxy, a minority called itself queer. Then, as it thought of itself as a community with a political project, as a new all-encompassing (revolutionary or reformist) agent, "queer" in turn became an identity of sorts.

There are good times ahead for queer discourse, because its proponents face an intractable contradiction between the part and the whole: they theorize as fundamental a domain (sexuality), thereby separating it from the rest, so they are always busy reconnecting. The multiplication of its social subjects ("woman," for example, melting into such strata as lesbian, butch/fem, transgender, color, etc.) and the impossibility of forming them into a coalition force "queer" to an ever-expanding and complex theorization. The greatest strength of queer theory in the radical milieu lies in the elusive nature of the concept: thanks to its ability to encompass everything, it acts as a unifying slogan, and the word functions as an intellectual marginality marker, a sign that recognizes authentic subversives. (In other quarters, it is "proletariat" that is being turned into a *fetish*, as Marx himself said at the Communist League's general council meeting, on September 15, 1850.)

☙

Whenever revolution is thought of as around the corner, breaking boundaries (sexual categories included) appears possible. In the early 1970s, people like the FHAR participants mentioned in chapter 7 were spontaneously "queer" before the word received its present meaning; because society in general was being called into question, they thought it possible to go beyond the (homo)sexual issue. With the ebbing of the tide, activism and theory had to make do with a changing situation. The (partial) success of the feminist, gay, and lesbian movements was also their (partial) integration into mainstream politics. "Queer" was a reaction against this, but the social critique was no longer there. Hence, on the one hand, a subtler integration (notably in the arts and academia), which everyone can visualize when the LGBT acronym is supplemented by the letter Q. On the other hand, an activism fueled by radicalism that is often and inevitably limited to verbal violence.

CHAPTER 12

Gay-Friendly, with Limits

Acceptance?

In 2015, the UK Annual Population survey found 1.7 percent of adults *self*-identifying as LGBT, 0.6 percent of whom declared themselves to be bisexual (at 5.5 percent, Lambeth was the gayest place in the UK). A US official census reports a "LGBT population" of 5 percent. The only real commonality between them is a declining but persistent social rejection. "What we do in bed is illegal in about half of the [US] States," Pat (now Patrick) Califia wrote in 1994. Over twenty years later, legal change does not mean equal treatment. Civil rights, busing, and affirmative action have not put an end to the inferior condition imposed on most people of color in the US. In a similar way, there remain motives for gays, lesbians, and transgender persons to mobilize and defend themselves. Inequity and exclusion compel gays and lesbians to meet among themselves in places that provide them with a minimum of protection, to share common experiences. This gives ample ground for both institutional and radical groups to organize and represent these still discriminated-against individuals.

Heterosex still prevails, but not like in 1970. Krupp's alleged homosexuality created a major scandal a century ago and possibly led to his suicide. Apple now has the highest market capitalization; in 2014, when its CEO announced that he was gay, there was no negative public response. It would not go down so easily for a warehouse worker employed in one of his outsourced companies. We tend to forget the limits of the evolution and how arduous the process has been; in the 1930s, Harry Whyte found it less difficult to "come out" in Stalinist Moscow (and later in Ankara) than in democratic London.

Post-war Britain was indeed giving gays a hard time, caught as they were between blackmailing gangs and police harassment. This was illustrated by the film *Victim* (1961), in which Dirk Bogarde played a bisexual lawyer who decides to give evidence in court against blackmailers, at the risk of destroying his career and incriminating himself.

Later, the purpose of decriminalization was certainly not to emancipate gays for freedom's sake but to adapt legislation to changing ways of life—often within narrow limits. The English 1967 law allowed for private sexual relations between consenting adults (only in England and Wales; Scotland waited until 1980 and Ulster until 1982). Yet the age of same-sex consent remained eighteen until 1994. Besides, the public/private definition was left to court and police discretion; a hotel room could be regarded as a public place. "The problem is that the State always wished the zone of privacy to be as narrow as possible," wrote Pat (now Califia) Califia. Things have certainly changed... maybe not entirely for the better. With the Internet, the private is the public, which allows for the permanent surveillance of anyone's personal life. It still is not simple everywhere in Spain, Italy, or Britain to live a gay life or as a gay couple. A lot depends on where you live: Cornwall's Penzance high street is probably less open-minded than London's Portobello Road, and gays are subjected to hate crimes in isolated rural areas of England.

Going back in time, when she was elected to the San Francisco Board of Advisors, Dianne Feinstein insisted on thanking "the gay community" for its part in her victory. That was 1969, the year of Stonewall. In her long subsequent career, Dianne did not do much to promote gay rights.

In order to protect themselves, lesbians and gays resorted to violence when it was necessary, *and also* built themselves up as an electoral force. When people fight for public existence, they need social and, therefore, political recognition. They cannot ignore laws or public institutions. This implies acting as a lobby. However, "accommodationists" will concentrate on lobbying and not do much else, whereas "anti-compromisers" will want to concentrate on the pressure of militant action to change legislation.

In 1975, Elaine Noble was the first openly lesbian candidate elected to the House of Representatives, with a platform that included homosexual rights. Four years later, 100,000 gays and lesbians marched in Washington. In 1987, 750,000 took part in the Great March, until that point probably the largest demo organized in the US capital. Jesse Jackson (an eminent figure of the civil rights struggle and a Democratic Party leader) joined in. So did Cesar Chavez (Latino organizer and head of the Chicano United Farm Workers), as did the president of the National Organization for Women (a moderate feminist group, rather white and middle-class). In Washington again, in 1993, a march for Lesbian, Gay and Bi Equal Rights and Liberation rallied nearly one million demonstrators. Even more than the increase in numbers, the nature and variety of the support testifies to the conjunction of gay and lesbian mobilization with the struggle for equal rights, i.e., for an end to legal and actual discrimination against blacks. Until then, the media had stressed the festive or provocative dimension of gay and lesbian actions; but, at this point, the press and TV made them appear respectable, with legitimate demands. Moreover, gays and lesbians started to be recognized as a political force that was part of the electoral equation. The "LGBT population" was becoming a political object. Bill Clinton was the first US statesperson of national caliber to add "gays" as an entity to the Democrats' traditional support groups: "the Jews," "the blacks," organized labor, united against the conservative religious right.

In the US there is no lack of churches—dissident or established—willing to make common cause with gay and lesbian demands; the first gay synagogue dates back to 1972, as does the first ordination of a gay priest by a major Christian church. When traveling across the United States in 1980, Guy Hocquenghem observed that "the real fabric of American gay life" was made of "basically non-political organizations [and] churches": gay Christians "are probably the first institution of the American homosexual community." For John Howard, in the late twentieth century, "Congregations were the strongest gay institutions in the state [of Mississippi]."

A historical stronghold of male privilege, the army is also a sensitive barometer of change—at a snail's pace. Since the 1991 Gulf War, the US Army has integrated woman soldiers into its combat units. Before being elected president in 1993, Clinton had promised to do away with the ban on gays and lesbians in the military: "We don't have a person to waste." An unkept promise. Still, equality is making slow, gradual progress in the military.

As for the police, we remember Carl Wittman calling San Francisco's gay neighborhood a "ghetto" because hetero cops were maintaining law and order. In Britain, in 2018, the British Stonewall LGBT group (founded in 1989 on the "acceptance without exception" principle) published its annual "Top 100 [LGBT friendly] Employers" list: it included the Cheshire Constabulary, Nottinghamshire, Leicestershire, and Northumbria Police, the Lancashire Constabulary, and Scotland Police (all better than University College London, which ranked at the bottom: number 98).

These are just quick probes into contemporary reality. Regarding the US, European public opinion (and sometimes radical thinking) overinterprets the most visible aspects, those presented by *parts* of the school system, the media, the university, and show business. John D'Emilio was probably right when, in 2016, he said that reading the *New York Times* or the *Chicago Tribune* today was not too different from looking at the pages of an "LGBT community paper." But political correctness only prevails on the surface of things. The blossoming of LBGT grassroots groups and institutions does not prevent the scales from being frequently tipped against the "progressive" camp. To mention just one example, in schools, heterosexuality (often marriage-related) remains central in sex education courses. The "alt-right" is not the only agent of backlash, particularly against women's rights. In Mississippi (population: 3 million), only one public hospital and one private clinic perform abortions. In Kentucky (over 4 million), *one* licensed surgical center offers abortion services. Worse, perhaps, various US states regulate the right to abortion in ways that discourage it. The United States of America qualifies as a politically incorrect and "reactionary" country on a number of counts—its prison population increased from three hundred thousand in the early 1980s to around 2.2 million today. (Incidentally, the female prison population in England and Wales more than doubled between 1995 and 2010.) Patriarchy in modern garb and straightforward everyday sexism are still going strong but are usually less self-assured, which often makes them more aggressive.

Back to our main subject: even if "gay business" contributed over $1.7 trillion to the US economy in 2017, the market does not liberate or put an end to gay bashing.

Out of the Closet into a "Ghetto"

Speaking in 1972 about his past as a trade union and French socialist party activist in the 1930s, Daniel Guérin declared:

> There were within me two men and two lives. In one
> life, I was exclusively an activist and in the other I was,

depending on the period, more or less tormented by my homosexuality, but there was never any link between my two selves. I certainly refrained from broaching the subject in front of any labor activists.... If other comrades were living with similar problems, it was only much later that I found out. There really was no interference between my two lives.

The divided homosexual self does not subsist in the twenty-first century as much as in the 1930s, but it has far from disappeared. There is more tolerance than acceptance, and open gay and lesbian social life exists on the margins, in closed circles that resemble ghettos, except now they are no longer repressed and clandestine. They have gained *visibility* (one of today's buzzwords), but what does that mean? Where and how are gays and lesbians visible?

Alix, in her thirties, lives in France, works as a nurse, and is a lesbian (she dislikes labels but rather likes this word). She does not mind telling her work colleagues about her sexual preference, and it has not caused her any trouble. However, asked if she could walk hand in hand with a woman she loves in a Paris street, first she said she is not very demonstrative anyway (an attitude now sometimes labeled "a-romantic"), but then added: "Yes and no. This is why we have those ghettos like the Marais [a cluster of streets in Paris center where a lot of gays meet]. All those bars and the neighborhood where you can allow yourself a true proximity, be yourself."

We met Fabrice in chapter 10. He pointed out a connection between sexual marginalization and class. The gay pickup spots he knows, in car parks or by a river, are seedy locations, "known essentially as fuck spots"; guys only go there "because there is no other way of meeting men and having a semblance of sexuality."

There, "class matters." Nothing prevents Fabrice from going to clubs in big towns and even gay-friendly bars, but that implies an hour's drive. Unlike the unattractive cruising spots, these are socially mixed, but mainly middle-class.

Of course, the Internet has changed the whole deal, even more so with smartphone apps: geolocation informs you about gays within a few miles radius. So it becomes possible for a gay worker to meet a gay boss "for a one-night stand," no more, "unless you believe in fairy tales," Fabrice said.

> In real life, once you've arranged a meeting, you're not in front of your screen with the multiple app filters, you don't face a picture and measurements, but a guy with all his social realities. And then it's not quite right any more.... But apart from that class question, at the beginning the Internet is great, you meet lots of guys, but you quickly find yourself on the brink of schizo-phrenia, because it completely alters your relationship to other people. Concretely, with your finger you scroll down guys' faces with a short description: height, weight—some even give the size of their penis—active, passive or both: so, it's hyper-codified. In the end it influences your own desire, you select certain crite-ria, you reject others. Actually, in the flesh, you realize these criteria don't hold water: you can meet some-body who's just the opposite and have a good time. Still, the Internet sort of formats you, it modifies the encounter, and even the sexual practices.

Fabrice lives in a small town:

> Because of where I live and how I live, it's pretty tough to find guys for fucking, but also simply to meet people with whom I can talk about real lives which have some-thing in common with mine, so I could feel less lonely. Where I live, there is nowhere I know I can meet homos, I have to go to the big town, eighty kilometers away. Today, despite all their limitations, these places are not

unimportant, they are necessary, even vital for some....
In lots of gays' lives, this is not a side-aspect.

Compared to early twentieth-century New York saloons (mentioned in chapter 3), which cared for the needs of homosexuals looking for mutual assistance and were similar to social clubs, the places Fabrice talked about have more to do with "survival," otherwise,

one would wonder why there are still so many cruising spots on the outskirts of every town, in so many remote dark corners.... They help alleviate a rather deep sexual misery, like to another extent more institutional gay-friendly places elsewhere.... In some situations, just hoping to find someone with whom you can share experiences over a drink, even that matters a lot.

The end of police harassment in cruising areas, Fabrice said, does not mean that everything is rosy now. Same-sex love is

something that is not lived out at all in the same way according to your social class and where you happen to be, in a town or in the middle of nowhere, how you live up to your sexuality, assert it and allow yourself to live your deep-down desires. There still are guys and women thrown out of home by their parents because of their sexuality. Quite a few others try to end their lives, and sometimes succeed.

Fabrice stressed the difference between cities and "the middle of nowhere," but Alix did not describe cities as lesbian heaven and used the word *ghetto* for Paris lesbians: "It's true there are places, whole towns which in theory allow you the freedom to live your homosexuality, but it gives an impression of slightly fake freedom, it's difficult not to be on the look-out, waiting for the insult, the little comment that will make you feel in hell."

There is no lesbian equivalent to San Francisco's Castro or Le Marais in Paris, Alix explained, because "for them [lesbians], a lot more happens underground … lots of parties, a few Paris bars, branched networks, lots of microcosms where a real lesbian culture is at work." By culture, she does not mean a specific mode of life, "rather a world of signs and cultural codes," for example, series like *The L Word*, which premiered in 2004, or *Orange Is the New Black*, first screened in 2013, which has had a worldwide audience. But "these are only representations…. Culture is not everything. It mostly emancipates the affluent classes. The success of these series is no proof at all of increased tolerance."

Imaginary Community

Asked about the existence of a lesbian community, Alix replied: "It may have been relevant thirty or forty years ago…. Today, with the Internet, the community is scattered, disseminated, ridden with contradictory struggles and aspirations."

If community means having something essential in common, what do all lesbians share? For Alix, the commonality is less a minority sexuality than "the need to face up to the challenge together and the pleasure of retrieving a form of solidarity." Maybe not a community, but "it resembles one. A community both effective… and virtual" that has more to do with image, culture, and media than reality: "There's never been such an abundance of pictures of gays on the screen, at the expense of what's left of past struggles, and of a true mobilization today."

When, in the 1960s and 1970s, same-sex love started being legitimate and socially acceptable, asserting and defending it initially gave birth to what looked like a cohesive identity; a common sexual orientation was seen to influence the lives of gays and lesbians more than all other aspects of their existence. With the decline of legal repression and social rejection in daily life, it has become clearer that a homosexual's life is determined by structural factors, above all, by his/her social position, but, paradoxically, his/her distinct sexuality has come to the fore more than ever, personally and publicly, and can be mistaken for an organizing factor. For the first time in history, a sexual singularity (today diversified in multiple categories) has "appeared" as a community.

In the 1920s, gay writers Wystan Hugh Auden (1907–1973) and Christopher Isherwood (1904–1986) would visit Berlin to connect with "their tribe." The constituents of "gay life" today are no less divergent than in 1930, and no homogeneity can be formed out of such heterogeneous components... except, as Fabrice and Alix pointed out, more acceptance comes with more awareness of harassment, while also creating more possibilities for solidarity. This combination of *increased acceptance* and *persistent resistance* gives the impression that a "community" exists.

There is a yawning chasm between the attempted *polysexuality* of the 1970s, as experimented with by the minority Lola Miesseroff mentioned in chapter 7, and today's banal reinvention of the couple (and the family) by gays, on the one hand, and the cruising areas described by Fabrice, on the other hand, as well as the extreme backroom sex of gay clubs, a distant equivalent of hetero swingers' clubs. Nothing too surprising in all this. Its relative normalization leads to a range of manners and attitudes for same-sex love that are as broad as the possibilities and constraints faced by the hetero majority, with a similar medley of competitive behavior, stereotyping of desire, conformism, and extravagance, all under the imperious pressure of class and money. Gays and lesbians now experience a mix of pleasure and misery similar to that experienced by the straights, albeit aggravated by what remains of forced marginalization. An accomplishment (sort of).

For the time being, let's leave the last word to a point made over thirty years ago:

> [T]o say "I am gay," "I am lesbian," or even "I am a paedophile… or sado-masochist" is to make a statement about belonging and about a specific stance in relationship to the dominant sexual codes. It is also to privilege sexual identity over other identities, to say in effect that how we see ourselves sexually is more important than class, or racial, or professional loyalties…. So there is a real paradox at the heart of the question of sexual identity. We are increasingly aware, theoretically, historically, even politically, that "sexuality" is about flux and change, that what we so readily deem as "sexual" is as much a product of language and culture as of "nature." Yet we constantly strive to fix it, stabilize it, say who we are by telling of our sex. (Jeffrey Weeks)

CHAPTER 13

Meanwhile, in The Rest of the World...

The evolution dealt with in this essay has occurred in the most dynamic and subjugating capitalist world, which in recent centuries has been coterminous with Western Europe and North America. (That could change with the rise of China.) Elsewhere, today, same-sex love is criminalized in eighty countries and punishable by death in half a dozen. In most of the world, "homosexuality" only exists where the progress of modernity makes it possible in big urban centers. A visible example is the organization of Gay Pride in cities like Tunis, Istanbul, and Beirut, with mixed success because of the violent hostility of the state, extremist groups, and reactionary segments of the population. Even Rio is not like it used to be (or was said to be). In 2017, over a million people gathered in the face of the city officials' opposition, but what does partying prove? In spite of its "liberated" sex life and "love hotels," Brazil has one of the highest rates of violence against gays and transgender persons in Latin America; in a single year, about 250 people were reported killed because of their sexual orientation. On the African continent, though some states like South Africa have recently decriminalized same-sex relations, they remain outlawed in more than thirty countries: Kenya, for example. According to Nigerian federal law, "carnal knowledge of any person against the order of nature" may result in up to fourteen years in prison—and twelve northern states include sharia in their criminal code. Most African countries oscillate between accommodation, repression, and a mixture of both, so the only safe places for gays are high-income residential areas or expat hotspots.

❧

Posterity sifts the past. In the late twentieth and early twenty-first centuries, the new vision of "same-sex" love that emerged in the US and Western Europe also changed the understanding of sexual matters in precapitalist times, and we tend to see today's less "advanced" capitalist parts of the world in light of our own contemporary point of view.

A few forays into the present and the recent past will suffice.

African Mine Marriages

In South African gold mines, from the 1930s to the 1950s, "mine marriages" would take place between an older man and a younger one, known as "husband" and "wife." Couples would invite each other to parties, where "the wife" served the guests. Sexually, the husband was "active," his wife "passive." In this patriarchal and gerontocratic society, the young were expected to care for the elders. As long as the arrangement remained discreet, white management accepted it; it was a stabilizing factor among a potentially restless manpower, and it reinforced the "native" seniority system outside the mine.

This lasted until the boy grew into a man in his mid-twenties.

> So men become "wives" in the mines in order to become husbands and therefore full "men" more rapidly at home.... The gender of their partner seems of less import than the overriding right [of mature men] to sexual congress. Furthermore, sexuality involves more than the physical act. It also involves a range of personal services. In this, "mine marriages" are clearly modeled on traditional rural marriage, with

the gender of the partner representing a fairly minor inconvenience. (T. Dunbar Moodie)

In that respect, "mine marriages" were not so dissimilar from hetero coupling. They decreased in the 1970s with the hiring of miners from other areas, who were interested more in "town women," prostitutes who had always been present on the outskirts of the compounds. This accompanied a general change. Rural black economy declined, proletarianized families lived less in the countryside, and when the home marriage system was shaken so was the "mine marriage" system; male sex started revolving more around town women and around squatter families, where "female" wives were closer to the men.

Turkish "Gender Consensus"

The Ottoman Empire decriminalized "sodomy" in 1858, and we saw in chapter 4 that gay ex-communist Harry Whyte chose to live in Turkey after the war. In the 1960s, James Baldwin travelled to Istanbul and spent extended periods of time in a country—undoubtedly sexist—where homosexuality is not a crime.

Nonetheless, modern secularized Turkey has always strongly disliked "the Ottomans' permissiveness about sexuality" (Kaya Genç, all subsequent related quotes are his). Ataturk's nationalist regime reinforced sex roles, locking women into a family role and expecting men to be good workers and soldiers: "gender had to be strictly defined following the modern Western model [and] signs of gender fluidity had to be repressed for the good of the nation. Over the 20th century, Turkish patriarchy, fused with paternalism, has solidified into a 'gender consensus.'"

Therefore, it comes as no surprise that official and unofficial repression should join forces against homosexuality. True, several opposition parties have nominated openly gay candidates, and "the main opposition party established a quota for neighborhood committee elections requiring that 1 in 5 candidates be gay." Besides, a first Gay Pride was authorized in 2003, and it numbered up to ninety thousand participants in 2014, but there have been none since, and the attempt to organize one in 2018 was met with tear gas and rubber bullets. LGBTI rights are trampled like human rights in general; May Day celebrations are also outlawed. According to Transgender Europe, Turkey has the highest murder rate of transgender people in Europe.

Not "the Real Thing"

A quick world survey shows the nearly universal reality of same-sex practices at the present time, but:

> Who is gay in an Indian context? What is gay? Who is homosexual? About three-quarters (72%) of truck drivers in North Pakistan who participated in a recent survey published in *AIDS Analysis Asia* admitted that they had sex with other males, while 76% stated that they had sex with female sex workers. Are these 72% gay? Homosexual? There is sufficient anecdotal evidence to indicate that in the other countries of the sub-continent, similar levels of male to male sexual behaviors exist as part of a broader sexual repertoire. Are these males bisexual?

> In South Asia,

> much same-sex sexual behavior involves non-penetrative varieties, mutually indulged in frameworks of friendships and sexual play…. 50 per cent of male university students recently interviewed in Sri Lanka reported that their first sexual experience had been with another man…. *Maasti* is a Hindi term which means mischief and often has sexual overtones when

it is used between young men.... Young men who culti-
vate such relationships do not consider themselves to
be "homosexual" but conceive their behavior in terms
of sexual desire, opportunity and pleasure.

In Indian culture, "sexual behavior in this context is rarely
seen as real sex, but as play." (Pierre Tremblay and Richard
Ramsay)

Only "as play," because *the real thing* takes place elsewhere, in man-woman relations within the family (which is
also the case with Gary Works hetero workers, as seen in chapter 10). The "Western" novelty of the late twentieth century
is that human reproduction (the production and rearing
of children) no longer necessarily coincides with a "man +
woman" couple, whereas the hetero family model still rules
in countries like India. (That might change in a few decades,
though.)

Western Myth and Oriental Reality

In Europe and North America, much is made of Indian
eunuchs and of intersex and transgender people, known
as *hijras*, some of them officially recognized as a "third
sex." Current opinion leans to the belief that they are able
to gain acceptance, find a place in society, and exist as relatively self-determining communities. In fact, in a country
where homosexuality was outlawed until 2018 and sexism
and homophobia still prevail, the hijra phenomenon is far
from breaking down oppressive identity taboos and barriers.
Most hijras suffer from discrimination and have a very low
status and a small income. Indian journalist Kal Friese wrote
that everyone "treat[s] the eunuchs and transgender people
known as hijras with fear, delight and respect. I suspect
this has a lot to do with the hijras' relentlessly theatrical
personas.... Overt sexuality isn't just tolerated in India, it is
demanded, but only within the safe confines of performance."

The hijra myth says a lot about Western love for a picturesque Orient, both ruthless and sexually permissive. It can be viewed as a late avatar of Orientalism—oddly paradoxical in the days of neocolonial and subaltern studies; the West, not without a patronizing attitude, continues to fabricate the East as an utterly different and fascinating world.

Moreover, an unmovable tradition-bound "East" does not coexist with an ever-evolving self-modernizing "West." The East does not live off an ageless culture. For example, in Qajar Iran, from the end of the eighteenth century to the early twentieth,

> standards of beauty were not gender-specific: male youths (*amrads*) as well as women were both deemed beautiful and sexually desirable by adult men, who were distinguished from the *amrads* by the marker of a full beard. By the end of the nineteenth century, however, love and erotic attraction became heterosexualized: beauty was now associated only with female femininity, while acceptable notions of male beauty and male same-sex love gradually disappeared. (Howard H. Chiang)

"Eastern" or non-European countries are ridden with tensions and conflicts that force them to question their ways of life and to invent their own pursuit of progress, for better or worse.

Time-Space Reinvented

Quite a few eighteenth-century Enlightenment philosophers depicted recently explored North American Indian or Tahitian societies as morally tolerant and sexually open, free of the constraints of modern civilization: so-called natural life provided a stinging critique of corrupt and decadent Europe. Later, critics of capitalism and class looked for inspiration (and sometimes models) in "primitive communism," characterized by egalitarian relations and common owner-ship. To resist and fight an overbearingly oppressive here and now, it is current practice to reinterpret former times or exotic todays. Anachronism and utopia are often a political necessity before a movement is strong enough to assert itself on the basis of its real content. When, in the 1970s, as our prelude briefly mentioned, US gays were tempted to see the "berdaches" as possible ancestors, and in so doing they were reading their present into somebody else's past.

Yet the past can also be a faraway present.

Richard Francis Burton (1821–1890), explorer, geographer, orientalist, polymath, and translator of the first English edition of *One Thousand and One Nights* had a deep interest in sexuality and erotic art. He never said he practiced same-sex love himself, but he conceived the notion of a "Sotadic" zone, where homosexuality (he used the word *pederasty*) was prevalent and celebrated; it covered large areas of Asia, small portions of Europe and North Africa, and all of the Americas. Calling it Sotadic—from the Greek poet Sotades, third century BC—again used ancient times as a reference point for homosexuality, as was the case with Engels, Bebel, Reich, and others in the nineteenth and early twentieth centuries.

❧

The same-sex practices documented in South African mines and in contemporary Asia, those analyzed by Burton, and those of the subcontinent hijras differ from "homosexuality" as it appeared in Europe and North America 150 years ago. In many societies, the gender separation (even segregation) of "man" from "woman" still matters at least as much as (or more than) sexual orientation—whether opposite-sex or same-sex.

CHAPTER 14

New Moral (Dis)Order

Our Goal and Method (slight return)

Only after our traveling in space and time, do the underpinnings of the subject-matter appear more clearly. We can now join the dots in a fragmented historical narrative and get a better picture by going back to elements dealt with earlier, especially in chapter 1.

In the nineteenth century, instead of treating man-man and woman-woman love as mere sexual relations—often repressed and always marginalized—the modern world invented "homosexuality" as a separate category, and then as a social question. Today, the extensive and intensive development of capitalist society enables us to grasp how deeply this has altered the way the sexes relate.

What we know as "homosexuality" is a particular category linked to the capitalist mode of production, which develops with this mode and, therefore, tends to extend globally but can only exist where capitalism deeply transforms social reproduction, family, sex relations, mores, and political life.

As explained in our prelude, this essay only deals with the supposedly most "advanced" parts of the capitalist world. (Japan is so distinctive that it had to be left out; it would warrant another study beyond the scope of this essay.) If we compared a world map of parliamentary regimes functioning more or less on the Western model with a map of countries where homosexuality is legal and relatively accepted, by and large one map would overlay the other. Between the legal equality granted to the citizen-elector and a tendency toward the equalization of sexual orientations, there is a connection, albeit not automatic, complete, or definitive (backlash effects occur, as proved by Germany in the 1930s). The more democratic capitalism is, the larger the scope for sexual variation. (Another map comparison would probably show that countries with a still strong tradition of arranged marriages are also those where modern "homosexuality" is unacknowledged or illegal.)

As seen in the previous chapter, in a whole array of cultures, the Christian world often standing as an exception, it is not illegitimate for two males to have sexual intercourse—on several conditions. They must maintain their social role (marrying and procreating). They must abide by a hierarchy between sexual partners, one of them playing the "active" (penetrative or "insertive") part, the other the "passive" (penetrated or "receptive") part. And the relation is only legitimate if between an adult and a young man or an adult with a man who behaves like a woman is supposed to.

From the eighteenth century on, parts of Europe slowly saw the emergence of a new historical category: men who have sexual relationships *only* with men. "As a starting point we have to distinguish between homosexual behavior, which is universal, and a homosexual identity, which is historically specific." (Jeffrey Weeks)

Family to Couple

Capitalism first developed under bourgeois rule (owners of capital frequently inherited by birth) who took advantage of habits of obedience and submissive attitudes, often with a strong religious tinge. You were taught to do as you were told by your father, husband, boss, and priest—all of them men. The industrial revolution reinforced gendered roles, including among the proletariat: misogyny and moral conservatism were rife in the labor movement (and have by no means disappeared). Proudhon's sexism is amply documented. Marx's daughters were brought up with the idea that their future husband should be the breadwinner and household head, and Eleanor only learned a proper trade because she was the family rebel. Daniel De Leon, leader of the US Socialist Labor Party from 1890 to 1914, was no exception. He adamantly maintained that the male worker must marry, and the wife must stay at home. Bourgeois puritanism was reflected in the morality of workers eager to prove that *they too* were "self-respecting decent people."

The old-style family was necessary in early capitalism: for the bourgeois, it guaranteed the transmission of assets; in the working class, laboring men and women pooled their labor power for family survival.

As the nineteenth century wore on, however, the deepening of the capitalist hold on society gradually gave a minor role to the rule of the father and rigid Victorian values. Unlike slavery, serfdom, and the various forms of agricultural and handicraft production, wage labor slowly allowed everyone (but men a lot more than women) a degree of autonomy from family and community bonds. As the wage is usually individualized, working away from home theoretically provides everyone, male and female—but in actuality more male than female—with an income that is his/her own.

This historical trend occurred earlier in England than in other countries. By the beginning of the nineteenth century, with the Industrial Revolution, it "was rare for fathers, mothers and children to work together in the same occupation. By the time of Napoleonic Wars, two thirds of married women were earning wages in such trades as retailing, lacemaking, brewing and spinning, a much higher proportion than in most of the world today." (Robert Tombs)

As more and more men and women were detached from a strict family-based economy and had to strike out on their own, sex began to move out of the traditional family orbit.

In the old days, for the real propertied class, as well as the petit bourgeois, founding and perpetuating a family meant the union of two lineages, which implied the necessity for both sides to control the choice of the marriage partner, and then for the husband to control the sexual life of his spouse. This age-old model has not vanished; it still exists in the bourgeois world, where passing on an estate can be an issue, but it no longer prevails in a society of individuals who choose their partners.

In England, before the Married Women's Property Act (1882), husband and wife became one person under the law, so the woman lost her legal identity—and her property rights. Then in 1882, the law recognized husband and wife as two separate legal entities, with the rights that entailed for both.

In France, until 1965, a married woman was "legally incapacitated."

Now, the two-parent (male and female) household has moved on to a couple that is the association of two autonomies who decide whether or not to perpetuate themselves in the form of children and, of course, whether to continue or terminate the coupling; an estimated 40 percent of UK marriages end in divorce.

In Western Europe, birth control developed in the eighteenth century with whatever means were available, but modern times have passed a tipping point with chemical contraception, legalized abortion (although legal does not mean easily accessible), and now delayed childbearing thanks to egg-freezing techniques.

We have experienced a double disconnection. First, generalized contraception dissociated sex from the risk of pregnancy. Second, procreation is now severed from sex: two people—or sometimes a single woman—can have a child without making love. Medically assisted procreation allows a woman-woman couple to raise a child without physical intercourse with a man. Surrogate motherhood makes it possible for a child to have three mothers: a genitor mother, a surrogate mother, and a social mother who will raise him/ her. A single man or woman now has the lawful right to adopt. In certain countries, an individual who has transitioned to a male gender identity (FtM) while keeping female reproduction organs can legally carry and deliver a child. Having a child used to be an event, sometimes an unwanted one; it now is a *right* people fight for—and get, to various extents—independently of their sex, sexuality, or couple/ single circumstances.

In Freud's days, the father was a problematic but overbearing presence. Nowadays, in the words of a character in a 2013 novel, "fatherhood is widely overrated." (A.S.A Harrison) "Parenting" challenges biological parenthood.

Homosexuality used to disturb a bourgeois order that included it in the nonreproductive sexualities (masturbation, adultery, and prostitution) and perceived it as a threat to a family as the basic social unit meant to produce future workers and soldiers (which entailed the repression of abortion; much later, with the decline of systematic pro-birth policies, abortion was made legal and became more socially acceptable). In the most "modern" Western countries, when the paterfamilias became obsolete and gays and lesbians proved to be good parents, a man-man or woman-woman couple fulfilled the family role just as well. Since it is no longer necessary to be a "mom and dad" family to raise children, send them to school, and prepare them for the world of work, i.e., to integrate them into present society, capitalism has no major problem with masculine or feminine homosexuality. In France, in 2017, there were 228,000 marriages, 7,000 of which were same-sex, and, in 2016, 192,000 civil partnership unions, 7,000 of which were same-sex. In the US today, two to eight million same-sex parents raise three to fourteen million children: the large discrepancy in figures is due to the different parameters chosen, but these statistics are enough to show that homosexual parenting is not a marginal phenomenon.

Nominally Equal Egos

The creation of a working class "free" to come onto the market where each proletarian sells his/her labor power also introduced a novelty: the advent of the individual.

Precapitalist society rested on fixed "natural" inequalities that were hard to modify or transgress: distinct groups had different duties, rights, privileges, and prohibitions, depending on sex, ethnic origin, free or servile position, noble or commoner condition, caste, region of birth, etc.

In contrast, we now live in a society of nominally equal egos, and the family structure has had to painfully adapt. A world where everyone has to sell his/her personal labor power also gives everyone the theoretical right over his/her own body and mind and, therefore, opens up the possibility for him/her to make his/her own life choices, sexual matters included. Whereas in the past very few same-sex-loving people cohabited as couples, twenty-first-century society is made of supposedly sovereign individuals who associate and choose their sex options, their ways of having and raising children, and even their own sex if they change what they were biologically born as (US figures for people transitioning in one degree or another vary from 700,000 to 1,300,000).

> In preindustrial America, heterosexuality remained undefined because it was truly the only way of life.... Free labor and the expansion of commodity production created the context in which a personal life could develop. Affection, personal relationships and sexuality increasingly entered the realm of "choice," seemingly independent and disconnected from how one organized the production of goods necessary for survival. Under these conditions, men and women

could fashion an identity and way of life out of their sexual and emotional attraction to members of the same sex. As industrial capitalism extended its hegemony, the potential for homosexual desire to coalesce into an identity grew. Not only had it become possible to be a lesbian or a homosexual: as time passed, more and more men could embody that potential.

Since the late nineteenth century, there have appeared men and women "for whom same-sex erotic interests became an organizing principle for their personal life." (John D'Emilio)

Love or sexual relationships between people of the same sex are still the experience of a minority, but it no longer goes against legal norms and social morality.

Capitalism knows no specific mores: it makes do with whatever does not impede its growth. Providing labor productivity and capital competition go on, the system is strong enough to rely on nothing else but its own laws. It leaves the individual a great deal of leeway in daily life, as long as he/she respects its fundamentals. In a deeply capitalized society, it is now discrimination between formally equal citizens that is punishable by law, including homophobia rather than homosexuality. "Normality" is what contributes to value-creating labor and the interests of the class that profits from it; instead of trying to impose a unique lifestyle, capitalist society potentially liberates all possibilities... that do not impede its functioning.

Capitalism dismantled the family to rebuild it as an association of individuals. The enlarged family of yesteryear, the village life where nearly all faces were familiar, has given way to the anonymity of the city, the nuclear family, the new stepfamily or blended family, and now the homosexual family. Individuals can remain single, meet one another, and socialize. The modern homosexual is an individual who has the option of being *only homosexual*, and perhaps living in one of the subcultures promoted by mass and diversified consumption.

(Freedom is problematic in a society where the individual completely depends on a social totality he/she neither controls nor understands. This predicament breeds what Christopher Lasch, fifty years ago, called "the culture of narcissism." Gender-bending, gender-blending, or a gender-quake will not do much to alleviate masculine and feminine role anxiety: "The more the self has become privileged socially and culturally, the more any confidence in the unity and certainty of the self has been undermined." (Laurence O' Toole) Perhaps this disorientation and disarray explain why a number of families explode into violence and murder: about twenty to thirty children are killed by their parents every year in Britain and as many as five hundred in the US. Another subject altogether, which we have no time to delve into here.)

(In)differentiation

When asked in 1784 what labor he wished to employ for the building of his Mount Vernon mansion, George Washington simply replied: "If they are good workmen, they may be from Asia, Africa or Europe; they may be Mahometans, Jews, Christians of any sect, or they may be Atheists." The US's first president selected workers on the sole criterion of competence... but as a slaveowner, he bought his slaves on the basis of *color*.

We do not live in a "pure" capitalist model, with a totally free worker meeting rootless capital on a labor market where every exchange occurs without any previous bond or bias. Capitalism inherits old hierarchies and creates those it needs, it divides and selects according to sex, skin color, nationality, and place of birth, and it reproduces differences, only erasing some by inventing others. Slavery is gone, but most US blacks still live in inferior conditions. Under capitalism, one human being is not worth the same as another.

The tendency toward indifferentiation is anything but linear and automatic. In nineteenth-century France, the mass hiring of women (45 percent of the textile labor force at the time of the First International) did little to decrease their submission to their husbands or their inferior social status. In the US, it was only in 1975 that the federal state stopped banning gays and lesbians from public jobs. Regarding race, interracial marriage was illegal in Mississippi until 1977.

In "modern" capitalist countries, the domineering father figure has certainly been on the wane for a long time, and same-sex marriage is now legal and gradually being accepted. Heteronormative pressure is weakening, but it is not disappearing; married or unmarried, hetero couples remain by far the majority. Furthermore, the increase in women working outside the home (in the US, 43 percent of union members were women in 2005) has not put an end to women's subordination.

"Reactionary" ideology and attitudes reflect a certain state of social reproduction, a state formerly unchallenged, still dominant in most regions of the planet, and still much alive in so-called progressive countries, as exemplified by the perseverance of US conservatism, which is trying to roll the moral clock back. Capitalism means an inherently unequal society. It does not equalize sexual practices; indifferentiation and hierarchization coexist and conflict with each other, in sexual matters as in others.

"In the Most Profound Sense, Capitalism Is the Problem" (John D'Emilio)

To get nearer to the crux of the matter… a few more words on identity politics.

One-sided Marxists reduce everything to class and interpret everything else as a consequence of the bourgeoisie vs. proletariat contradiction. As a result, sexual emancipation is theorized as a mere aftereffect of the abolition of wage labor.

(This usually comes with a determinist streak. Human evolution is cut down to a succession of modes of production, like a railway line sequence where one station leads to another. The train is often late, sometimes even derailed, but ultimately the proletariat will reach the terminus. Tunnel vision. Some people like the future to be foretold.)

As to the identity concept: its most perceptive supporters do not do away with class altogether. They build up a cross-over theory that does not refute Marx but defuses him. They maintain the importance of class domination but complete it by adding other dominations, which de facto alters a class perspective into one that is multigroup. The explain-it-all proletariat of ossified Marxism is replaced by numerous mutually complementing agents of change. (Relative proportions of added components and degrees of dilution depend on which partner is prioritized.)

Only history provides the litmus test. The emergence and transformation of "sexuality" in the past two hundred years prove class to be the constant and sex/gender the variable. This does *not* mean that class creates everything. It means that class determines the general evolution of sexuality, to a large or small extent depending on the direct or indirect impact of the capital/labor relation: more direct in New York than Palermo in 1900, and in Gary, Indiana, than in Addis Ababa today. The historical narrative we have covered, especially in chapters 1 and 2, demonstrates that "class analysis" stands the historical test of time for explaining the chain of events, the causation. (On another related matter, in the evolution of twentieth-century South Africa, from the early days of industry and mining to apartheid and its demise, the "race" factor, however crucial it was, only played its part under the influence of labor/capital relations.)

Much of the debate hinges on what is meant by "domination" and "exploitation." There are numerous forms of domination: boss over wage earner, man over woman, parent over child, adult over youth, teacher over student, doctor over patient, citizen over foreigner, white person over person of color... Not all are the result of the exploitation of the proletarian by the bourgeois. While the capitalist mode of production structures the modern world, it does not cause everything that happens; for instance, it did not invent the subordination of women.

In a world where capitalism rules, however, it is this system that reproduces and modifies the past and the present according to its logic, notably the subordination of women, even (however little change there is) in Saudi Arabia, a "reactionary" but eminently capitalist country.

The challenge is to grasp *at the same time* how the labor/capital relation determines the world *and* by which forms (variable in time and space) of domination this relation asserts itself: in other words, to understand *what links* domination and exploitation, as well as *what makes them diverge*. Critical theory aims to simplify by addressing the complex, not by negating complexity.

First, capitalism cannot exist without exploiting the proletarians. Second, not every particular oppression or discrimination is structurally indispensable; some decrease or fade away, others are born or reborn, and others still are enhanced. The essential domination is none other than *bourgeois domination*, the preservation of which shapes the other forms of domination. What the capitalist class needs is to secure its foundation: the separation between labor and the means of production, but also the whole of social reproduction, which involves the family, although, of course, not the same family everywhere and at all times. Societies have long repressed (or marginally tolerated) practices that we now call homosexual to safeguard the family as it existed at the time. A sexuality decoupled from reproduction was too disturbing for nineteenth-century bourgeois to admit its public manifestations, the expression of which was quickly banned as *pornographic.* Flaubert and Baudelaire were taken to court in 1857 for *Madame Bovary* and *Flowers of Evil* respectively. In 1889, London publisher Henry Vizetelly spent three months in jail on account of thirteen offensive translations from the French, including eight Zola novels and an English version of—again—*Madame Bovary*, translated by Eleanor Marx. Free love and "trial marriage" were objectionable topics in 1900, while a hundred years later they are mainstream practice: sex before and outside wedlock (there are now more unmarried than married couples in the US), the pill sold as a prescription drug, explicit claims to sexual pleasure for men and women, up to and including the homo-compatible family.

Maintaining exploitation is indispensable to capitalism; repressing one form or another of sexuality is not.

Unequal Homosexuality

"Perverts are all created equal," according to a character in the Japanese film *Love Exposure*. We are doubtful about perverts, but equality between gays and lesbians is very far off.

All human groups have to ensure their own reproduction, which entails in one way or another managing people's bodies, especially those that carry and deliver children, i.e., female bodies. In present society, ruled by production for value, the production of children is socially regulated, less under direct control by men (father, husband, etc.) and more indirectly managed by public health institutions and social services.

Equalizing (relatively, we repeat) sexual practices does not bring about sexual equality between men and women. The same evolution that has led to an accommodation with homosexuality has transformed the subordination of women but not abolished it. If the twentieth century brought with it the option of living outside the heterosexual family unit, men have benefited from it a lot more than women, who are still under the constraint of a specific production: delivering children and taking care of them. Because the woman remains associated with motherhood and everything that comes with it, she is still treated as a social inferior, only in gentler ways than before. Lesbians, also being women, are publicly less visible than gays and no more their social equal than other women compared to men.

At the 2017 Paris Gay Pride, only one float out of eighty was specifically lesbian, which seems odd if we think of the blossoming of lesbian associations in France. When asked about this, Alix explained that "the event that gets the most lesbians together in Paris is the Wet for Me party," which has been organized every year since 2008, where "one thousand women gather to have fun, with DJs, music… militancy is not their forte." Not much in terms of visibility.

Gay and lesbian erotic/pornographic film mail-order catalogues illustrate how double standards die hard in same-sex love. The same company provides gay customers with films focused on the most physical aspect, on virility and power, and it offers its lesbian clientele films where beauty and tenderness prevail. Penises and tough looks for boys; bare shoulders and smiles for girls. Hardcore vs. softcore. The male body is penetrated; the female body is caressed. Granted, there are exceptions—gays are allowed their share of romance too—but, basically, it's sex for men and love for women. Here again, nothing surprising in the persistence of stereotypes: there is no reason why homosexuality should be immune to socially dominant sexual codes. Sex is *not* a great equalizer.

Managing the Confusion of Feelings

Unlike traditional societies that impose a sex model, only tolerate deviation if it remains inconspicuous, and, in fact, often repress it, a society of individuals equal before the law generates a blossoming of lifestyles, notably of varied sexual orientations free to constitute their own little worlds.

Apart from the majority hetero couples, alternate models develop, officially recognized yet often only half socially accepted. In 2017, the German Federal Constitutional Court ruled in favor of the option of having a "third sex" or "gender" (different from male or female) on birth certificates or other legal documents. Germany was the first European country to make the change; no doubt others will follow. As long as I abide by its laws, the state no longer requires me to fit in with a "binary" definition of human beings. All identities are welcome—which does not mean socially equal—providing the police can check my identity on my ID card... and soon with biometric identification sensors.

Contemporary capitalist society not only has to enforce moral commands and prohibitions, which still exist, but must also to ensure the coexistence of a plurality of models based on the best interests of the system's reproduction and the continuity of bourgeois domination. Previously, the rulers forced the ruled into a one-size-fits-all pattern and pretended it worked. Today's conundrum is to manage a multiverse of overlapping and conflicting standards.

In the most "progressive" parts of the world, the old moral order is replaced by a diversity of mores that fragment sexuality ad lib and ad infinitum. Beside a still dominant hetero yardstick, there is such a profusion of categories that it calls for ever-expanding acronyms. The LGBT world does its best to keep up with this accelerated compartmentalizing. In "LGBTQQIP2SAA," for example, "2S" means "Two Spirit" (formerly called "berdache"; We'wha is at last recognized for what he/she was), and the second "A" designates allies. To avoid missing an unexpected group, it is advisable to add "+" or "*," which leaves the door open to a new subdivision, otherwise, that latecomer would be rendered invisible.

This is as much a coalition as a stage where each group competes for its share of the limelight. If all minorities are equal, some are more minority than others, so visibility conditions their existence. Probably a lost battle; the list will never be inclusive enough, and the best possible inclusivity will always leave out some community.

The Straight's Predicament, or Heterosex Deconstructed

An unexpected section to conclude a study on homosexuality… or maybe not. Our essay deals as much with sex as with same-sex love. As seen in chapters 1 and 2, "heterosexuality" and "homosexuality" are not timeless absolutes; they were invented at the same time.

Nothing can be safely taken for granted anymore.

The transformation of the contemporary family has a bearing on "mainstream" or majority man-woman sexuality. In a 2015 survey, one-third of Americans younger than thirty declared they were not heterosexuals, a figure that is only relevant as a symptom of how modern society pictures itself.

In the past, when "hetero" mores were so obviously the norm, they did not require a specific definition and did not even come with a label of their own. Now LGBTQQIP2SAA people are not the only ones concerned with sex- or gender-fluidity. In its own still privileged way, heterosex now translates into a multiplicity of subgroups. To name but a few: heteroflexible, allosexual, sapiosexual (attracted to a partner's intellect), pansexual, aromantic, halfromantic or panromantic, lithromantic (in love with no particular desire to be loved in return), skoliosexual (attracted to individuals—male or female—unattached to the masculine/feminine opposition), omnisexual, asexual, nongender, hyposexual/hypersexual, androsexual, androgynosexual, autosexual, halfsexual, graysexual, petplay (self-identifying with one's favorite animal), and monosexual (just me). Not forgetting the altersexual people, who are, admittedly, "confused" about their sexual preference. (Though unwelcome in gender-speech, the "sex" denotation is definitely striking back.) Polyamory is the art of loving several people at the same time, but with no concern about gender, hence possibly heteronormative. Quite a few of these subdivisions have their own flags, some a variation on the LGBT rainbow. The cyberworld allows for LDR (long distant relationships). BDSM (Bondage Discipline Dominance Submission Sadomasochism) is a world of its own, which cuts across a broad range of the above and is increasingly being democratized: handcuff sex toys can be bought from respectable mail-order catalogues. The Saturday night porn movie of the 1970s has been replaced by porno chic and intellectualized, innocuous S and M.

Of course, there is nothing new in all those inclinations, stimulations, and activities. In the early twentieth century, ethnic and sexualized modern urban zones—called "moral regions" by Chicago sociologist Robert Park in *The City* (1925)—served as meeting places for a marginal fringe, tolerated but scorned by established society. In contrast, contemporary sex subcultures publicly display an ever-expanding diversity of self-proclaimed milieus, small or large, coexisting and intermingling, endlessly labeling and categorizing themselves, produced by the modern combination of "free" individuals and "social" networks.

We have drifted light years away not only from Victorian values but from the rules of conduct that prevailed in 1920 or 1950. The unmentionable—i.e., sex, whatever wording is used—was whispered about in privacy or confined to the pages of a diary; it is now exposed in full view. Psychiatrists had the privilege of elaborating complex patterns to separate the "normal" from the "deviant." Today, everyone is welcome to find his/her own way of situating his/her emotions and yearnings within the wide range of existing classification, or even to invent a new category. The repressed is now—and, indeed, must be—expressed. The question, however, is: What is changed and gained in the process? If we enjoy far-reaching sensual and erotic autonomy, why do we need so many behavioral crutches, why this overload of psychologists, therapists, counsellors, helpers, coaches, etc.?

Early modern times imposed a one and only type of sex life, or at least a certain façade of family attitudes. *Bland new world* capitalism goes so deep that its domination accepts all models that contribute to its reproduction. Yet the chief constraint is stronger than ever; we have to find a place within the labor/capital relation. Apart from that, just as we are free to swing from one political party to another, we have the right to select our personal niche, associate with fellow members, move on to the next one if we wish—every slot being defined by its difference from its neighboring ones—and even find a name for it.

Modern (wo)man realize that it can be as destabilizing to have to choose one's affective niche as to abide by fixed norms. The mix of overlapping affiliations makes it even worse, as it proves that none of these elusive categories create any true belonging.

Heterosexuality was unmarked, because it was the norm: as others (gays, lesbians, etc.) now have markers, being a majority is not enough. These are crisis times. It is now the straights' turn to subdivide, classify, and make do with flagrantly divided selves.

Heterosexuality still rules, but...

Polysex

"How can you define yourself while claiming at the
same time your universality and your difference?"
—Line Chamberland

In a not too distant past, anyone with "different" sexual
practices had to hide them. Nowadays, he/she looks for legal
defense and protection and turns this difference into an identity organized into a specific group. At best, an omnipresent
capitalism leaves each of us with the option of having his/her
own space wherein he/she can live his/her sexuality without interference. *At best...* Against this backdrop, it is hard
for radical critique to imagine how the situation could be
overcome by a polysexuality that today seems as utopian
as the overthrow of wage labor, the state, and classes. What
the situationists called the society of "separation perfected"
cuts off work from the all other activities, production from
consumption, toil from leisure, and creates a series of space-
times each devoted to its own special function, particularly
that reserved for sex, which exists as a reality set apart, a
taboo, yet ever-present, a phobia as much as a fascination,
obsessed by performance.

No wonder, then, that the practice of an activity so essential and now so constrained and split up could fuel dreams of
universal harmony free from tensions and conflicts; everyone would love (and make love with) everybody, and every
desire would be mutually shared and, therefore, immediately

satisfied. Something akin to the play world of commercials, except it would be for real: the "sexual revolution" at long last accomplished, sex games with no risk of loss, Sade without crime, Fourier's "lecherous fantasy" without the cumbersome procedures of his phalanstery, painless masochism, hedonism now available to every one of us, "no neurosis, lots of synthesis, no perversity (since that will be absorbed into a new, more healthy sexuality), and even more verbal posturing." (Pat [now Patrick] Califia) This is clearly not what we are talking about, nor was it Carl Wittman's, the FHAR's, or Mario Mieli's perspective.

"We do not have to determine or limit in advance the forms of possible or desirable sexual relationships. Chastity itself is not to be rejected. It is a perversion as commendable as another!" (*A World without Money*, 1975–1976)

"We have nothing against perversions. We are not even opposed to heterosexual monogamy for life." (*La Banquise* no. 1, 1983)

To each according to his/her excitability.

Now comes the time to explain one of the excerpts at the beginning of this essay. In Steven Shainberg's film *Secretary* (2002), Lee, a young borderline woman inclined to self-harm and recently out of hospital, starts working as a secretary for an attorney, Edward. They do not "have sex" but engage in soft dominant/submissive relations, and she obeys every order Edward gives her, such as performing her secretarial tasks with both hands tied behind her back. At the same time, Lee has an uninspiring boyfriend, Peter, and is even close to marrying him. Eventually, Edward commands her to sit motionless in his office chair until he returns. He does not come back for three days, but Lee obediently sits and waits. When Peter visits her during this "ordeal," he is utterly baffled and shocked: "Is this… sexual?" he asks, and this is when she replies: *"Does this look sexual to you?"* Lee and Edward will finally marry but keep alive their erotic roleplay of bondage, dominance, and submission. (As far as we can see, engaging in S and M has delivered her from self-mutilation.)

Lee's retort is spot-on: she answers a conventional question by inquiring into the heart of the matter. She refuses to be slotted into a behavioral category. Indeed, what is "sexual" and what is not? Lee and Edward do not "have sex"—that only happens at the end of the story—so a "sexuality quiz" would have trouble qualifying their relationship.

In 1950, it was taken for granted that heterosex was the "one best way." It no longer is, at least not to the same extent, and this is positive, but a real change would include a transformation of the relation between sexuality and the rest of life. However, a world without what we have known for a century and a half as "(homo)sexuality" cannot be imagined today.

It is a platitude to say that love/sex is laden with contradictions, as expressed among others by Baudelaire when he wrote in his *Lesbos* poem: "Love will laugh at Heaven as it laughs at Hell." What is less banal is to understand how most societies—including capitalist society, with its contemporary "political correctness"—have tried to rid themselves of this ambivalence by devising impracticable moral rules.

Consequently, if we have often used the word *homo*, short for *homosexual*, which is now obsolete and pejorative compared to *gay*, it is because of the richness and ambiguity of the word *homo*, which means *same* in Greek and *human species* in Latin. Sometimes etymological blurring is the symptom of a meaning to be discovered. "Love has to be reinvented," Rimbaud wrote in 1873 (since then, we've experienced many a "season in hell"). This would be no less than inventing a world where I could be *human* without the obligation to be classified as homo, hetero, bi, etc., i.e., without the need to find shelter by fitting in with persons who I believe are *the same* as me.

Interview with Gilles Dauvé

Your Place or Mine **challenges contemporary perceptions of class and gender and provides a truly novel critique of sex identities, creating a radical theoretical framework that challenges capitalism and the state. What was the inspiration for writing the book, and why did you feel it was necessary to publish it now?**

This book only exists because "sex/gender" became a social issue at the end of the twentieth century. As a friend of mine born in 1979 said, "From the point of view of social progress, it is possibly the only issue that would allow you can make a good case for serious improvement in my lifetime." With "lots of limitations," he added. Still, it has given birth to important struggles.

Let's briefly go back in time. Precapitalist societies rested on fixed inequalities; distinct groups had different functions and rights depending on sex, ethnic origin, free or servile position, etc. With the advent of capitalism, the family ceased to be the dominant economic unit. Now, each male and female proletarian is "free" and forced to sell his/her *own* labor power, works outside the home, and wages are usually paid to the individual, which gives him/her (men a lot more than women) more scope for personal choice in his/her life, which also results in a higher degree of autonomy in sexual matters. Factory work made women's collective struggles more frequent and much larger. Instead of same-sex love remaining individual or marginal, it became more of a group phenomenon.

Only in the last decades of the twentieth century did this evolution become stronger and more visible. This was not a linear trend, of course. It was more manifest in the US than in Poland, for example, yet overall gender relations changed because of structural changes in the capital/wage labor relations.

This is what most radical gay, lesbian, queer, etc. critiques find hard to accept. Probably because radical milieus, even when they share a "class analysis," generally partake of what could be called a "Foucauldian" mindset: capitalism is seen as a combination of domination, control, and ideological mechanisms, among which the class factor is only one, or is even a mere consequence.

What is capitalist society based on? History shows that class relations—and class confrontations—structure modern society. Gender does not. Nor does race, but that would require another book. Our society is founded on the prole-tarians—of whatever gender—having to earn money to live and, therefore, having to submit to productive labor. Class is not the only form of discrimination and oppression. Others play their part, but none is structurally indispensable to the running and continuation of capitalism: depending on the time and place, present society preserves, modifies, or alle-viates them. In this sense, "class" is a constant, "gender" a variable. So we won't get rid of gender oppression by simply adding gender struggles to class struggles; the class structure is the focal point that determines historical evolution.

You were part of publishing the radical gay magazine *Le Fléau Social* in the 1970s. What was that experience like? How does the work that appeared in the magazine compare to transgressive writing on sex and sexuality today?
Let's remember that in the late 1960s and early 1970s, the French gay and lesbian movement was not on a scale compa-rable to that in the US: no Paris Stonewall! At the time, when

Le Fléau Social crossed paths with libertarian communism and the Situationist International (which had just dissolved itself in 1972), the social surge brought about by the 1968 general strike was still alive but was on a downhill slope. When I met Alain Fleig, he was already fairly isolated, and he was writing most of the magazine himself. On the one hand, his critique of gay "reformism" (limited to acceptable demands against discrimination) resulted in his rejection by mainstream gays. On the other hand, his insistence on sex/gender as an issue came too early for "Marxists," who failed to grasp the importance of the issue.

Soon after we met in 1973, we decided I'd write a piece on "the women's question." Alain Fleig chose the title, "Feminism Illustrated," and the subtitle, "Diana's Complex", which he inserted between two pictures. One portrayed two women arm-in-arm, not necessarily lovers yet obviously romantically involved. The second picture showed straight-faced marching Red Army women, probably from Russian civil war times. He said these two utterly opposed visions typified two diametrically and equally misleading ways to women's emancipation: the illusion of the intrinsic subversive power of love/sex and ensnaring women as soldiers for a cause they had no control over. (This essay is now available in English: https://blastemeor. noblogs.org/files/2018/10/Feminism-illustrated-2018.pdf.)

The article came out in what was to be the last issue of *Le Fléau Social*, which sold well, but a rebellious time was gradually closing in, and the magazine folded. Alain realized that he'd have to wait for global emancipation, and he did not believe in partial emancipation; a born provocateur, he had no patience for political, or even gay, activists, recognition-seekers, left-wingers, Trotskyists, Maoists, trade unionists, national liberation war supporters, counterculture followers, etc. As he did not fit in with what was to become the LGBT world, he took up other pursuits and worked as a photographer and art historian till his death in 2012.

Le Fléau Social was "queer" in all but name, and, above all, with no attempt to advocate for a new subversive identity… in the name of a critique of all identities.

Can you talk a little about the fragmenting of gay identities? Do you see the LGBT+ movement as a cohesive movement? In the beginning, the belief in "a common cause" was inevitable—and indeed necessary. In their early days, the 1960s and 1970s rebels hoped that their assertion and defense of same-sex love would be sufficient to bring *all* gays and lesbians together. As one of the first French gay groups said, "Homosexual political militancy transcends membership in any social class, ideology, or party." Later, it became increasingly obvious that a gay, lesbian, or transgender person's life is determined by structural causes, above all, by their social position, which bears heavily on how they can live out their sex/gender singularity. Alix, the young lesbian interviewed in the book, describes how incohesive "the community is, scattered, disseminated, ridden with contradictory struggles and aspirations."

Now, most Western Europe and American towns have an active LGBT+ group, and a number of countries have anti-homophobia laws. But let's not delude ourselves. Society has certainly changed a lot in the last fifty years: for instance, though we may not think of Serbia as a particularly gay-friendly country, an openly lesbian politician was elected prime minister in 2017—and she attended Pride. That doesn't mean that a male or a female couple can publicly walk hand in hand on a Belgrade street without fearing harassment. Very few do in "safer" London, actually. A minor matter? Possibly, but this fact, and thousands of more important ones, amply demonstrate that we still live in a predominantly homophobic—and sexist—world. It's this combination of *increased acceptance* and *persistent resistance* that gives a "community" the impression that it exists.

How has the quest for respectability and assimilation changed the face of gay politics?

When gays and lesbians abandoned whatever revolutionary goals they'd had, it was inevitable that they'd try to speak to and for all homosexuals and fight for visibility and legal rights. The critique of bourgeois/hetero marriage logically gave way to a demand for same-sex marriage. Basically, this is a demand for equality.

Fighting against gender (or color) discrimination is absolutely necessary, which does not mean that a radical critique necessarily emerges from these movements. In fact, it rarely does.

"Class struggle" does not mean constant class conflict. Even when struggles are reformist, which most of them inevitably are, labor struggles do not fight for *equality* between the wage earner and the bourgeois; the employee can very rarely become his/her employer's equal by becoming a boss him/herself. On the contrary, gays and lesbians, when fighting *as gays and lesbians*, fight to be treated the same as straights, and quite legitimately so, which is tantamount to demanding *sexual equality*. This request, contemporary society can meet, though only in some countries and within limits.

Besides, when the real working class fails to meet the revolutionaries' expectations, Marxists tend to fine-tune the class concept, tiresomely differentiating and dividing strata. Similarly, the belief in a sex-based commonality has shifted into a search for multiple identities. "Gender" is deemed too exclusionary: there are now four "main" genders, and globally seven, or twenty-two. What *Le Fléau Social* could not foresee in 1975 is how much the gay movement was to become part and parcel of identity politics, and the trouble with identities is we can never embrace and include enough of them.

Can you talk about the research that went into writing *Your Place or Mine*?

On the sex/gender subject, it was difficult to choose from among an abundance of books, articles, testimonies, archives, etc. My concern was to go back to history: Robert Bleachy on Berlin, George Chauncey on New York, John Howard on the US South, Dan Healey on Russia... also, Elisabeth Lapovsky-Kennedy and Madeline Davis on lesbian life in the 1940s.

Some books from the 1970s and 1980s, like those of Jeffrey Weeks or John D'Emilio, have been more inspirational than a lot of recent research. I am afraid these writers are now regarded as worthy pioneers... yet a bit outdated, too "class-oriented" in the eyes of academics specialized in women's, gender, and subaltern studies.

One last name: Anne Balay—both an activist and a scholar, she wrote a stimulating book on gays and lesbians in a steel mill. She related events without trying to make a point, *yet* her study is grounded in a strong analytical framework. I'd say there's more *theory*—and relevant theory—in her book than in many other overrated books.

Do you think it's possible to create a world where one can be *human* without having to be classified by sexual practices or gender expressions? How do we undo the pervasive labeling and fragmenting of identity that has distracted from broader issues of class?

As long as capitalism exists, we will live in a world of competing identities: national, religious, ethnic/racial, etc. Up to now, proletarians have rarely been able to act as a social group with *"radical chains,"* a group large and cohesive enough to overthrow the whole system but also universal enough to go beyond separate categories, i.e., a group "which cannot emancipate itself without emancipating all other spheres of society." This was how communists defined the proletariat in the 1840s.

Nearly two hundred years later, we're instead witnessing the opposite: practically and theoretically, the emphasis is not on the universal—what and who holds society together—but on the particular, the various separate constituents of the whole. Capitalism is currently addressed as an addition of crisscrossing dominations.

Alas, combining distinct agendas does not help them converge.

Pushing the boundaries of identities, however, becomes possible when, for instance, cleaners, most of whom are women, some of them undocumented people of color, go on a strike that fuses wage demands, immigrant questions, and gender issues—a small example, but one that allows us to begin to go deeper into the heart of the matter.

For the moment, we're not done with distinctions and labeling.

So, you think "revolution" is not in the offing: Then what about struggles taking place "here and now?"
I've never advocated "all-or-nothing" or "only-revolution-will-do" politics.

Despite my reservations about same-sex marriage, I obviously supported it against reactionary forces. When abortion rights are denied, or when they are trampled upon in countries where they're legal, the US, for example, I and my friends naturally take to the street to defend them. Just as I marched against the new French labor law a couple of years ago, supported a cashiers' strike, the Yellow Vests in 2019, and was part of a small-scale demo last month to uphold underage immigrants' rights.

Taking part does not imply misinterpreting these actions as an automatic step to overall change.

That being said, I do not face the world as a prophet and tell it: "Give up your present struggles, they're partial, choose the real true ultimate struggle instead." I merely try to explain why partial struggles are taking place and how that situation could change. Till then, I suppose this book might be too class-focused for some radical gays, and too sex- or gender-related for a number of diehard Marxists. Well... I can only quote Kafka: "We should read only those books that bite and sting us."

Note on the Book

This essay, first written as a series of articles in French on the DDT21 blog (https://ddt21.noblogs.org) (2016–2017), was turned into a book by Niet! and published in 2018 as *HOMO. Question sociale et question sexuelle de 1864 à nos jours*.

The present English version has been extensively rewritten. In particular, the chapter on "reactionary masculinity" in Germany in the first decades of the twentieth century has been left out and the chapter on Russia is completely new. Also, only short passages of the three interviews with ex-FHAR member Lola, the contemporary lesbian Alix, and the gay man Fabrice have been translated into English. For easier readability, nearly all books and articles referenced below are in English.

Further Reading

General Works

Chauncey, George, Martha Vicinus, and Martin Duberman, eds. *Hidden from History: Reclaiming the Gay and Lesbian Past*. New York: New American Library, 1989.

D'Emilio, John. "Capitalism and Gay Identity." In Henry Abelove, Michèle Aina Barale, David M. Halperin, eds. *The Lesbian and Gay Studies Reader*. New York: Routledge, 1993.

D'Emilio, John, and Estelle B. Freedman. *Intimate Matters: A History of Sexuality in America*. Chicago: University of Chicago Press, 1998.

Herdt, Gilbert, ed. *Third Sex, Third Gender: Beyond Sexual Dimorphism Culture and History*. Brooklyn, NY: Zone Books, 1993.

Miller, Neil. *Out of the Past: Gay and Lesbian History from 1869 to the Present*. New York: Vintage Books, 1995.

Tamagne, Florence. *A History of Homosexuality in Europe: Berlin, London, Paris 1919–1939*. New York: Algora, 2004.

To the best of our knowledge, only extracts from Charles Fourier's *New Amorous World* have been translated into English, but his *Theory of the Four Movements* (1808) gives us glimpses into his perception of sex/love: "instead of trying to correct the passions," let's "try and discover [their] dynamics." https://libcom.org/files/Fourier%20-%20The%20Theory%20of%20the%20Four%20Movements.pdf.

Bibliography

Prelude: We'wha in Washington

Berry, David. "'Workers of the World Embrace!' Daniel Guérin, the Labor movement and Homosexuality" (2004). https://libcom.org/files/4799.pdf.

Désy, Pierrette. "The Berdache: "Man-Woman" in North America," (1978). http://classiques.uqac.ca/contemporains/desy_pierrette/the_berdaches/the_berdaches_texte.html.

Faiman-Silva, Sandra. "Anthropologists and Two Spirit People: Building Bridges and Sharing Knowledge" (2011). https://tinyurl.com/2ndk9r8r.

Goldman, Emma. "The Unjust Treatment of Homosexuals (1900–1923)." http://www.angelfire.com/ok/Flack/emma.html.
A short informative compilation of her statements on the subject.

Kissack, Terence. *Free Comrades: Anarchism and Homosexuality in the US 1895–1917*. Oakland: AK Press, 2008. https://tinyurl.com/5h73k7e8.

Timmons, Stuart. *The Trouble with Harry Hay*. Modesto, CA: White Crane Press, 2012 [1990], chapter 10.

"Two-Spirit." *Cultural Anthropology*, chapter 10: "Sex and Gender." https://courses.lumenlearning.com/culturalanthropology/chapter/two-spirit.

Chapter 1: The Invention of "Sexuality"

Foucault, Michel. *The History of Sexuality, Volume 1: The Will to Knowledge*. New York: Pantheon Books, 1978 [1976]. https://suplaney.files.wordpress.com/2010/09/foucault-the-history-of-sexuality-volume-1.pdf.
When caught up in the post-1968 turmoil and its succession of strikes and factory occupations, Foucault gave more positive importance to class than he later would. His early 1970s lectures stressed the link between the modern prison and a capitalism based on measuring and managing time. The length of the sentence was time-adjusted depending on the severity of the crime, as the wage is calibrated in the context of productive work time: "Capitalist power clings to time, seizes hold of it, makes it purchasable and usable," Foucault explains.

The "prison form" and the "wage form" are "historically twin forms";
see The Punitive Society: Lectures at the College de France 1972–1973,
London: Picador, 2018. *As working-class struggles receded, like many
other temporary Marxists, Foucault's interest decisively moved from
production relations to control mechanisms and from class analysis
to discourse analysis. This new "master narrative" was in tune with
the times.*

Freud, Sigmund. "'Civilized' Sexual Morality and Modern Nervous Illness,"
(1908). https://sexualityandthemodernistnovel.files.wordpress.
com/2017/02/freud_sexualmorality.pdf.
*Without going into too much detail, it is worth mentioning that
Wilhelm Reich (and later Freudo-Marxism) turned Freudianism upside
down. Freud and Reich both gave sex a central role in how society
functions. Freud described sex as a powerful creative force and as a
potential destabilizer that civilization must acknowledge and keep
under control. Reich also believed that society was based on sex but
drew the opposite conclusion: social oppression is rooted in sex, therefore, sexual emancipation would bring down social oppression.*

Freud, Sigmund. *Three Contributions to the Theory of Sexuality*. Journal
of Nervous and Mental Disease Publishing Company. New York: 1910
[1905]. https://www.stmarys-ca.edu/sites/default/files/attachments/
files/Three_Contributions.pdf.

Halperin, David. "Is There a History of Sexuality?" (1989). https://
programaddssrr.files.wordpress.com/2013/05/is-there-a-history-
of-sexuality.pdf.

Katz, Jonathan Ned. *The Invention of Heterosexuality*. Chicago: University
of Chicago Press, 2007.
This text was written in 1990, but only published in 1995.

Marr, Andrew. *A History of Modern Britain*. London: Pan Books, 2008,
part 1.

Praz, Mario. *The Romantic Agony*. Oxford: Oxford Paperbacks, 1970 [1933].
*An abundant compilation of the erotic sensibility, imagery, femme
fatalism, neurosis, etc. found in nineteenth-century literature.*

Williams, Patricia J. "Bad Blood. The History of Eugenics in the Progressive
Age." *Times Literary Supplement*, July 20, 2018. https://www.the-tls.
co.uk/articles/history-of-eugenics-in-progressive-age-book-review-
patricia-williams.
The article reviews: Ladd-Taylor, Molly. Fixing the Poor: Eugenics
Sterilization and Child Welfare in the Twentieth Century. Baltimore:
John Hopkins University Press, 2017. *Because eugenics had its
infamous Nazi side, we tend to overlook how influential it was in
democratic America and social democratic Scandinavia, albeit with a
major difference. Eugenics is indeed the science and practice of "people
selection" to preserve, restore, or improve the social order. However,
Scandinavian and US social hygiene policies aimed at regulating
the working population; Nazi racial hygiene aimed at eliminating
segments of the population.*

Von Krafft-Ebing, Richard. *Psychopathia Sexualis*. London: Forgotten Books, 2012 [1886; followed by numerous other editions]. https://ia801603. us.archive.org/0/items/PsychopathiaSexualis1000006945/ Psychopathia_Sexualis_1000006945.pdf.

Also of interest is the Thomas N. Painter collection held by the Kinsey Institute, which consists of sixty-one bound volumes and ninety-nine archival folders.

Chapter 2: The Invention of "Homosexuality"

Bleachy, Robert. *Gay Berlin: Birthplace of a Modern Identity*. New York: Alfred A. Knopf, 2014.

D'Emilio, John, and Estelle B. Freedman. *Intimate Matters: A History of Sexuality in America*. Chicago: University of Chicago Press, 1998.

Engels, Frederick, "The Book of Revelation" (1883). https://www.marxists. org/archive/marx/works/subject/religion/book-revelations.htm.

Katz, Jonathan Ned. *The Invention of Heterosexuality*. Chicago: University of Chicago Press, 2007.

Kennedy, Hubert. "Johann Baptist von Schweitzer: The Queer Marx Loved to Hate." *Journal of Homosexuality* 29, nos. 2–3 (February 1995).

Kennedy, Hubert. "Karl Heinz Ulrichs: First Theorist of Homosexuality." In *Science and Homosexualities*. Edited by Vernon Rosario, 26–45. New York: Routledge, 1997. https://hubertkennedy.angelfire.com/ FirstTheorist.pdf.

The frequent tendency of Marxist translators and publishers to soften Marx's and Engels's language is particularly noticeable on the subject of same-sex issues and results in bowdlerized versions of their texts. There's no point ignoring that, by and large, same-sex issues were one of Marx's and Engels's blind spots. With a well-thumbed handbook of quotes as their main guide, some Marxists tend to read themselves into Marx and reinvent him as a feminist, an ecologist, etc.

Before gays and lesbians started revisiting the past, Schweitzer's infamous side belonged to the dustbin of history and only his dictatorial habits were remembered. In the early twentieth-century socialist milieu, Lenin's opponents would accuse him of "Schweitzerism" when they argued he was trying to rule over the party as an autocrat. In her critique of Lenin's "ultra-centralism," Rosa Luxemburg does not mention Schweitzer's name but refers to the "dictators" at the head of the ADAV.

Luxemburg, Rosa. "Organizational Questions of the Russian Social Democracy" (1904). https://www.marxists.org/archive/luxemburg/ 1904/questions-rsd/index.htm.

Takacs, Judit. "The Double Life of Kertbeny" (2004). http://www.policy. hu/takacs/pdf-lib/TheDoubleLifeOfKertbeny.pdf.

Chapter 3: What Is "A Man"? Of *Fairies* and *Men* in New York

Berry, David. "'Workers of the World Embrace!' Daniel Guérin, the Labor movement and Homosexuality" (2004). https://libcom.org/files/4799.pdf.

Carpenter, Edward. *Civilization: Its Cause and Cure*. London: George Allen & Unwin, 1921 [1890]. https://www.gutenberg.org/files/44094/44094-h/44094-h.htm.

Carpenter, Edward. *Love's Coming of Age*. New York: Mitchell Kennerley, 1911 [1896]. https://archive.org/details/lovescomingageao2carpgoog.

Chauncey, George. *Gay New York, 1890–1940*. New York: Basic Books, 1994.
A lot more than the title suggests: a reflection on what gay identity and community are and are not.

Coleman, Jonathan E. *Rent: Same-Sex Prostitution in Modern Britain 1885–1957*. Lexington: University Press of Kentucky, 2014. http://uknowledge.uky.edu/cgi/viewcontent.cgi?article=1022&context=history_etds.

Cook, Matt. *London and the Culture of Homosexuality 1885–1914*. Cambridge: Cambridge University Press, 2003.

Dauvé, Gilles. "On the 'Woman Question'" (2016). https://troploin.fr/node/88.
An overview of the evolution of women's condition.

D'Emilio, John, and Estelle B. Freedman. *Intimate Matters: A History of Sexuality in America*. Chicago: University of Chicago Press, 1998.

Freud, Sigmund. *Three Contributions to the Theory of Sexuality*. New York: Journal of Nervous and Mental Disease Publishing Company, 1910 [1905]. https://www.stmarys-ca.edu/sites/default/files/attachments/files/Three_Contributions.pdf.

Guérin, Daniel. *Autobiographie de jeunesse. D'une dissidence sexuelle au socialisme*. Paris: La Fabrique, 2006 [1972].

Hollinghurst, Alan. *The Sparsholt Affair*. London: Picador, 2017.
A novel that spans seven decades of same-sex life in England.

Howard, John. *Men Like That: A Southern Queer History*. Chicago: University of Chicago Press, 2000.

McKenna, Neil. *The Secret Life of Oscar Wilde*. New York: Arrow Books, 2004.
An excellent biography of a master of self-invention, a quality that contributed to his social downfall.

O'Sullivan, Emer. *The Fall of the House of Wilde*. London: Bloomsbury Publishing, 2016.
On Oscar Wilde's larger than life family as much as on Oscar himself.

Chapter 4: Sexual Engineering in Moscow

Figes, Orlando. *A People's Tragedy: The Russian Revolution 1891–1924*. New York Penguin, 1996.

Foucault, Michel. *History of Madness*. Milton Park, UK: Routledge, 2006 [1961].

On "the great confinement" in seventeenth- and eighteenth-century Western Europe.

"Harry Whyte: The Gay Scot Who Challenged Stalin." KaleidoScot, May 31, 2015. http://www.kaleidoscot.com/harry-whyte-the-gay-scot-who-challenged-stalin-3405.

Healey, Dan. *Homosexual Desire in Revolutionary Russia: The Regulation of Sexual and Gender Dissent.* Chicago: University of Chicago Press, 2001.

Contrary to some translations that tone down Gorki's anti-homosex stand in 1934, he did not call for the end of "homosexuality" as a practice but for the elimination of "homosexuals," i.e., of human beings.

Hiller, Kurt. "An Early Activist Critique of Stalin's 1934 Antihomosexual Law: 'A Chapter of Russian Reaction.'" MRonline, January 5, 2015. https://mronline.org/2015/01/05/hiller050115-html.

Kollontai, Alexandra. "Theses on Communist Morality in the Sphere of Marital Relations" (1921). https://www.marxists.org/archive/kollonta/1921/theses-morality.htm.

Lenin, V.I. "The Taylor System—Man's Enslavement by the Machine" (1914). https://www.marxists.org/archive/lenin/works/1914/mar/13.htm.

Stites, Richard. *Revolutionary Dreams: Utopian Vision and Experimental Life in the Russian Revolution.* Oxford: Oxford University Press, 1989.

Whyte, Harry. "Can a Homosexual Be a Communist? Harry Whyte's Letter to Stalin" (1934). https://thecharnelhouse.org/2015/06/27/can-a-homosexual-be-a-communist-harry-whytes-letter-to-stalin-1934.

Zetkin, Clara. "Lenin on the Women's Question." https://www.marxists.org/archive/zetkin/1925/lenin/zetkin2.htm.

Chapter 5: Sexual Reform in Berlin

Bebel, August. "On Homosexuality and the Penal Code" (Reichstag speech, 1898). https://www.marxists.org/archive/bebel/1898/01/13.htm.

———. "Woman and Socialism" (1910 edition), chapter XII, § 5: "Crimes against morality and sexual diseases." https://www.marxists.org/archive/bebel/1879/woman-socialism/index.htmEduard.

Bernstein, Eduard. "The Judgement of Abnormal Intercourse" (1895). https://www.marxists.org/reference/archive/bernstein/works/1895/wilde/homosexual.htm.

Bleachy, Robert. *Gay Berlin: Birthplace of a Modern Identity.* New York: Alfred A. Knopf, 2014.

That the anti-homosexuality § 175 targeted only males was no sign of a more lenient attitude toward lesbians but, rather, a legal aspect of the long history of writing women out of the public sphere; they were supposed to be sufficiently controlled by tradition, morals, and family pressure. In 1909, there was an attempt to extend § 175 to women, but the scheme failed.

Goldman, Emma. "The Unjust Treatment of Homosexuals (1900–1923)." http://www.angelfire.com/ok/Flack/emma.html.

Extracts from a 1923 article to the Scientific-Humanitarian Committee's Yearbook.

Gordon, Mel. *Voluptuous Panic: The Erotic World of Weimar Berlin*. Port Townsend, WA: Feral House, 2006.
For those fascinated by Berlin decadence in Weimar times.

Halifax, Noel. "Richard Linsert and the First Sexual Liberation Movement." *Socialist Worker*, May 3, 2017. http://socialistreview.org.uk/420/richard-linsert-and-first-sexual-liberation-movement.

Isherwood, Christopher. *The Berlin Stories*. Cambridge, MA: New Directions Publishers, 2008 [1946].
A collection of semiautobiographical texts about his life in Berlin in the 1930s, which inspired Bob Fosse's film Cabaret *(1972).*

Kessler, Harry. *Journey to the Abyss: The Diaries of Harry Kessler 1880–1918*. New York: Vintage Books, 2013.

"Lubbe, Marinus van der 1911–1934." libcom.org. http://libcom.org/history/articles/1911-1934-marinus-van-der-lubbe.

Pfemfert, Franz. *Die Aktion*, March 1912. Cited in Irène Cagneau. *Sexualité et société à Vienne et à Berlin 1900–1914. Discours Institutionnels et controverses intellectuelles dans Die Fackel, Die Aktion, Der Sturm, Pan, Die Zukunft*. Villeneuve d'Ascq, FR: Presses Universitaires du Septentrion, 2014.
Die Aktion (1911–1932) started as a critical art and literary magazine, opposed the war in 1914, and became one of the main mouthpieces for radicals and left antiparliamentarian communists.

"The Politically Expedient Scapegoat: Accusations of Homosexuality as a Tool of Defamation in Weimar and Nazi Germany." The Expedient Scapegoat, August 27, 2010. https://expedientscapegoat.wordpress.com.

Reich, Wilhelm. *Mass Psychology of Fascism*. New York: Farrar, Straus and Giroux, 1980 [1933], chapter 7.
Not to put too fine a point on it, another quick word on Reich. Like Frederick Engels, Reich returned to Ancient Greece and explained away female and male homosexuality as a means to evade the fetters of family and marital life (chapter 3): "In terms of the drive's energy, passive homosexuality is the most effective counterpart of natural masculine sexuality, for it replaces activity and aggression by passivity and masochist attitudes, that is to say, by precisely those attitudes that determine the mass basis of patriarchal authoritarian mysticism in the human structure."

Weiss, Andrea. *In the Shadow of the Magic Mountain: The Erika and Klaus Mann Story*. Chicago: University of Chicago Press, 2008.
Focused on Klaus and his bisexual sister but also a history of the Mann family. Klaus Mann committed suicide in 1949. His long autobiography (The Turning Point: Thirty-Five Years in This Century) *says nothing about his homosexuality: "the most essential things are the unspeakable ones." (Letter to his mother, 1942)*

Lack of space prevents us from studying the "reactionary masculinity" movement that was active in Germany from the end of the nineteenth century to the Nazi seizure of power. For insight into its contradictions and politics, see: Oosterhuis, Harry, and Hubert Kennedy, eds. *Homosexuality and Male Bonding in Pre-Nazi Germany*. Milton Park, UK: Routledge, 1992. The book is a collection of articles from *Der Eigene* (1898–1932), probably the first homosexual magazine.

Chapter 6: Butch/Fem, or the Rise and Decline of the Woman Worker Image

Anderson Kelly. "Amber Hollibaugh Interviewed by Kelly Anderson." Voices of Feminism Oral History Project, 2003–2004, New York. https://www.smith.edu/libraries/libs/ssc/vof/transcripts/Hollibaugh.pdf.
Born in 1946 in a "poor white-trash" family, Amber describes herself as a "lesbian sex radical" and "high femme dyke." She has been involved in the civil rights movement, the anti–Vietnam War agitation, leftism, feminism…

Chamberland, Line, *Mémoires lesbiennes. Le Lesbianisme à Montréal entre 1950 et 1972*. Montréal: Éditions du remue-ménage, 1996.

Chamberland, Line. "Montréal: 1950–1977. La visibilité lesbienne et l'importance des butchs et des fems." In Christine Lemoine and Ingrid Renard, eds. *Attirances. Lesbiennes fems, lesbiennes butchs*. Paris, FR: Éditions Gaies et Lesbiennes, 2001.

Goodloe, Amy. "Lesbian Identity and the Politics of Butch-Femme" (1993). http://amygoodloe.com/papers/lesbian-identity-and-the-politics-of-butch-femme.

Hickey, Alyssa. *Feminist and Lesbian Relations in Buffalo, New York, and the Nation during the 1970s*. History Theses 28, 2014. https://tinyurl.com/26efskf4.

Lapovsky-Kennedy, Elisabeth, and Madeline D. Davis, *Boots of Leather, Slippers of Gold: The History of a Lesbian Community*. New York: Penguin, 1994.
Some readers have regretted that the narrative was skewed toward "the butch side." It is true that fems tend to be less vocal than butches. Is this simply one more example of masculine public image dominance? On their method, see Davis, Madeline D., and Elisabeth Lapovsky-Kennedy. "Oral History and the Study of Sexuality in the Lesbian Community: Buffalo, New York, 1940–1960." *Feminist Studies* 12, no. 1 (Spring 1986): 7–26. https://www.jstor.org/stable/3177981?seq=1#page_scan_tab_contents.

Krupat, Kitty, and Patrick McCreery, ed. *Out at Work: Building A Gay-Labor Alliance*. Minneapolis: University of Minnesota Press, 2001.

Nestle, Joan. *The Persistent Desire: A Femme-Butch Reader*. New York: Alyson Books, 1992.

Chapter 7: "To Be What We Do Not Know Yet": Stonewall and the Aftermath

Chatterley, Constance, and Gilles Dauvé. "Feminism Illustrated" (1974). https://blastemeor.noblogs.org/files/2018/10/Feminism-illustrated-2018.pdf; "40 Years Later: A Conversation with Constance" (2015), https://blastemeor.noblogs.org/post/2018/10/22/feminim-illustrated-english-translation-available.
Discusses the magazine Le Fléau Social.

D'Emilio, John. *Sexual Politics, Sexual Communities: The Making of a Homosexual Minority in the United States, 1940–1970*. Chicago: University of Chicago Press, 1998.

Italy 1977–8: Living with an Earthquake (pamphlet). *Red Notes*. http://libcom.org/files/IMG-Italy1977-8-Red%20Notes.pdf.

Lauritsen, John. *The First Gay Liberation Front Demonstration*. GayToday.com. http://gaytoday.com/viewpoint/011904vp.asp.
First-hand testimony about Stonewall from a left-wing activist.

Mieli, Mario. *Homosexuality and Liberation: Elements of a Gay Critique*. Translated by David Fernbach. London: Gay Men's Press, London, 1980 [1977]. https://tinyurl.com/2tyjc2cr.

Miesseroff, Lola. ENTRETIEN/Explosons les codes sexuels ! Une ancienne du FHAR parle. DDT21. https://ddt21.noblogs.org/?page_id=1769.
The series of articles that inspired the present book included this interview with former FHAR member Lola Miesseroff. Only short passages have been translated here. For French readers, we recommend her documentary history of "radical" people and events immediately before, during, and in the couple of years after May 1968: Voyage en outre-gauche. Paroles de francs-tireurs des années 68. *Montreuil, FR: Libertalia, 2018.*

NOT BORED! "Proletarians of All Nations: Caress Yourselves!" http://www.notbored.org/caress-yourself.html.

Thorstad, David. "Guy Hocquenghem on Homosexual Desire, Capitalism, and the Left." MRonline, April 21, 2011. https://tinyurl.com/56hnn8ze.
A review of Guy Hocquenghem's Screwball Asses *that cites Jeffrey Weeks.*

Wittman, Carl. *Refugees from Amerika: A Gay Manifesto*. The Red Butterfly (1970). http://library.gayhomeland.org/0006/EN/A_Gay_Manifesto.htm.
Translated from Gulliver *no. 1 (1972).*

Wolf, Sherry. "Stonewall: The Birth of Gay Power—an excerpt from Sherry Wolf's book, *Sexuality and Socialism*." *International Socialist Review* 63 (January 2009).

Chapter 8: Impossible Identity

D'Emilio, John. *Sexual Politics, Sexual Communities: The Making of a Homosexual Minority in the United States, 1940–1970*. Chicago: University of Chicago Press, 1998.

D'Emilio, John, and Estelle B. Freedman. *Intimate Matters: A History of Sexuality in America*. Chicago: University of Chicago Press, 1998.

Kissack, Terence. *Free Comrades: Anarchism and Homosexuality in the US 1895–1917*. Oakland: AK Press, 2008. https://tinyurl.com/5h73k7e8.

Lorde, Audrey. "Age, Race, Class and Sex: Women Redefining Difference" (1980). In Anne McClintock, Aamir Mufti, and Ella Shohat, eds. *Dangerous Liaisons: Gender, Nation, and Postcolonial Perspectives*. Minneapolis: University of Minnesota Press, 1997. https://archive.org/details/dangerousliaisonooooounse/page/n5/mode/2up.

Miller, Neil. *Out of the Past: Gay and Lesbian History from 1869 to the Present*. New York: Vintage Books, 1995.

As a concept and an inspiration for sex rights activism, *gender* expresses as many contradictions as it helps to resolve. Or possibly, as a GenderQueer said, "gender is so very fundamental that we don't have language for it"; cited in Krupat, Kitty, and Patrick McCreery. ed. *Out at Work: Building A Gay-Labor Alliance*. Minneapolis: University of Minnesota Press, 2001. The rise of this word, which I will not go into here, deserves a study in its own right. Please read the last note in Dauvé, Gilles. "On the Woman Question'" (2016). https://troploin.fr/node/88.

Chapter 9: Gender and Genre: The Paradox of Gay Culture?

Highsmith, Patricia. *Her Diairies and Noteboks, 1941–1995*. New York: Liveright Publishing Corporation, 2021.

Schenkar, Joan. *The Talented Miss Highsmith: The Secret Life and Serious Art of Patricia Highsmith*. New York: Saint Martin's Press, 2009.

Epstein, Rob, and Jeffrey Friedman, dir. *The Celluloid Closet*. London/New York: Channel 4 Films/HBO Pictures, 1995.
Includes an interview of Farley Granger, one of the actors in Strangers on a Train.

Murray, Raymond. *Images in the Dark: An Encyclopaedia of Gay and Lesbian Film and Video*. New York: Plume Book/Penguin, 1996.
The reader will not agree 100 percent with the author... a wealth of information all the same.

White, Edmund. *Le Flaneur: A Stroll through the Paradoxes of Paris*. London: Bloomsbury, 2001, chapter 5.
Edmund White's quality as a biographer casts more than a shadow of a doubt on the notion of "gay culture": his detailed research on Jean Genet's life (1993) amply demonstrates that Genet's sexual inclination was only one dimension among many of the writer and certainly not enough to typify him. White's own evidence belies his viewpoint.

Wilson, Andrew. *Beautiful Shadow: A Life of Patricia Highsmith*. London: Bloomsbury, 2003.

"Gay/lesbian" categorizing is inadequate for artistic works that cross other lines. Peter Strickland's film *The Duke of Burgundy* (London: Film4

Production, 2014) is as much an "S and M" as a "lesbian" film: Which label should we prioritize? Better to admit that both are inadequate.

D.H. Lawrence was neither gay nor were his themes, but *Women in Love* (New York: Thomas Seltzer, 1920) undoubtedly dealt with male love between Rupert and Gerald. "There was a pause of strange enmity between the two men, that was very near to love.... This they would never admit" (chapter 12). "[O]f course he had been loving Gerald all along, and all along denying it" (chapter 16). After Gerard's suicide, the novel ends on a conversation during which Rupert tells his wife Ursula he loves her but he "wanted eternal union with a man too: another kind of love."

Ursula disagrees: "You can't have two kinds of love. Why should you?"

"It seems as if I can't," he said, "yet I wanted it."

"You can't have it because it's false," she said.

"I don't believe that," he answered."

This dialogue also concludes Ken Russell's excellent film inspired by the book: *Women in Love* (Los Angeles: Brandywine Productions, 1969).

In *Rupert and Gerald*, a short story probably written around 1916 and a sort of forerunner to *Women in Love*, D.H. Lawrence brought out Birkin's attraction to men: "[A]lthough he was always drawn to women, feeling more at home with a woman than with a man, yet it was for men that he felt the flushing, roused attraction which a man is supposed to feel for the other sex.": published in Alberto Manguel and Craig Stephenson, eds. *In Another Part of the Forest: Anthology of Gay Literature*. London: HarperCollins, 1994.

Should we shelve *Lady Chatterley's Lover* in "General Fiction," and *Women in Love* in "Gay and Lesbian Fiction"? At the end of the day, one wonders if the tenets of "gay culture" do not, in fact, mean works that to some extent support LGBT+ rights, which is not the case with *Women in Love* or Patricia Highsmith's novels, so they don't qualify.

Barry, Sebastian. *Days without End*. London: Faber and Faber, 2016.

In the above-mentioned—and very good—*In Another Part of the Forest: Anthology of Gay Literature*, Alberto Manguel and Craig Stephenson thought it necessary to point out in the introduction that "the notion of gay literature is guilty on two counts: first, because it implies a narrow literary category based on the sexuality of either its authors or its characters; second, because it implies a narrow sexual category that has somehow found its definition in a literary form. And yet the notion of a 'gay literature,' albeit recent, doubtlessly exists in the public mind." Over twenty-five years later, this is all the more true; see, e.g., Woods, Gregory. *A History of Gay Literature: The Male Tradition*. New Haven, CT: Yale University Press, 1999.

Chapter 10: Being Gay or Lesbian in the Workplace

Allison, Dorothy. *Skin: Talking About Sex, Class and Literature*. Ann Arbor, MI: Firebrand Books, 1994.

Balay, Anne. *Steel Closets: Voices of Gay, Lesbian, and Transgender Steelworkers*. Chapel Hill: University of North Carolina Press, 2014.

Dauvé, Gilles. *White Riot, 1922: Race & Class in 20th Century South Africa* (2018). https://theanarchistlibrary.org/library/gilles-dauve-white-riot-1922.
    Addresses the division between proletarians, with special reference to race.

Embrick, David G., Carol S. Walther, and Corrine M Wickens. "Working Class Masculinity: Keeping Gay Men and Lesbians Out of the Workplace." *Sex Roles* 56, nos. 11–12 (June 2007). https://tinyurl.com/2p883zh6.
    This is an example of a preferred academic subject matter: working-class homophobia.

Krupat, Kitty, and Patrick McCreery, eds. *Out at Work: Building a Gay-Labor Alliance*. Minneapolis: University of Minnesota Press, 2001.

McShane, Steve. "The Magic City of Steel." U.S. Steel Gary Works Photograph Collection, 1906–1971, Indiana University, 2010. http://webapp1.dlib.indiana.edu/ussteel/context/essay.jsp.

Pannekoek, Anton. "Party and Working Class" (1936). https://www.marxists.org/archive/pannekoe/1936/party-working-class.htm.

Prole.info. *The Housing Monster*. Oakland: PM Press, 2012.

For the percentage of women in the various sectors of the working population in Canada, the US, and Europe, see "Women in Male-Dominated Industries and Occupations (Quick Take). Catalyst, updated October 29, 2021. http://www.catalyst.org/knowledge/women-male-dominated-industries-and-occupations.

For more detailed US figures on gender, race, and work, see "Labor Statistics from the Current Population Survey." US Bureau of Labor Statistics, updated January 20, 2022. https://www.bls.gov/cps/cpsaat18.htm.

For former FHAR member Fabrice's full interview in French, see "'Aujourd'hui y a plus moyen !' entretien avec Fabrice." DDT21. https://ddt21.noblogs.org/?page_id=1851.

In the interview mentioned in our bibliography for chapter 6, Amber Hollibaugh reminds us that homophobia is often denounced where it is the most visible, which is often in working-class milieus. Sexual prejudice (as well as racist bigotry) is more openly voiced by what used to be called the lower classes than by the educated middle classes, so it is much easier to spot and blame. "Prolophobia"?

Chapter 11: Queer, or the Identity That Negates Identities

Allison, Dorothy. "A Question of Class." History Is a Weapon. http://www.historyisaweapon.com/defcon1/skinall.html.

Baroque, Fray, and Tegan Eanelli. *Queer Ultra-Violence: Bash Back! Anthology*. San Francisco: Ardent Press, 2011. https://tinyurl.com/2ph2u62h.
Misguided theory, yet very informative about the activities of Bash Back! and Radical Queer.

Butler, Judith. *Gender Trouble: Feminism and the Subversion of Identity*. Milton Park, UK: Routledge, 1990. https://selforganizedseminar.files.wordpress.com/2011/07/butler-gender_trouble.pdf.

———, *Notes toward a Performative Theory of Assembly*. Cambridge, MA: Harvard University Press, 2015.

Califia, Pat [now Patrick]. *Public Sex: The Culture of Radical Sex*. Hoboken, NJ: Cleis Press, 1994.

Duggan, Lisa, and Dan H. Hunter. *Sex Wars. Sexual Dissent and Political Culture*. Milton Park, UK: Routledge, 2006 [1995].

Howard, John. *Men Like That: A Southern Queer History*. Chicago: University of Chicago Press, 2000.

Kornak, Jacek. *Queer as a Political Concept*. Thesis, Helsinki University, 2015. https://helda.helsinki.fi/bitstream/handle/10138/152620/queerasa.pdf?sequence=1.
Kornak's thesis provides a useful synthesis of the issues addressed in this chapter.

Mennel, Barbara. *Queer Cinema—Schoolgirls, Vampires, and Gay Cowboys*. New York: Columbia University Press, 2012.

"Paul Goodman: The Politics of Being Queer, 1969" (extracts). https://tinyurl.com/6d4zzv2w.
Paul Goodman (1911–1972), a bisexual pacifist and anarchist, developed a queer humanism vision whereby gay sexual encounters are "acts of liberation," with the "democratizing" effect of "throwing together every class and group": "I have cruised rich, poor, middle class, and petit bourgeois; black, white, yellow and brown … and once or twice cops." Crossing class barriers, however, is not breaking them down.

Paul B. Preciado, in the French daily *Libération*, September 2, 2014. *He gave an excellent summary of a basic queer creed: "Yesterday, the place of struggle was the factory, today it is the body and the subjectivity." (Libération, July 28, 2018) Author of* Counter-Sexual Manifesto *(first published in French and Spanish in 2000), a classic and cult book of queer theory (English edition by Columbia University Press).*

QED: A Journal in GLBTQ Worldmaking. Michigan State University Press. http://msupress.org/journals/qed.

"The Queer Nation Manifesto." History Is a Weapon. http://www.historyisaweapon.com/defcon1/queernation.html.

Chapter 12: Gay-Friendly, with Limits

Berry, David. "'Workers of the World Embrace!' Daniel Guérin, the Labor Movement and Homosexuality" (2004). https://libcom.org/files/4799.pdf.

Dearden, Basil, dir. *Victim*. London: Allied Film Makers, 1961.

Dirk Bogarde (1921–1999) often played characters with an "inappropriate" sexuality: The Servant (1963), Death in Venice (1971), Night Porter (1974)… *Social pressure forced him to keep silent about his homosexuality to nearly the end of his life.*

Hocquenghem, Guy. *Un journal de rêve. Articles de presse (1970–1987).* Paris: Verticales, 2017.

Stonewall. "The Full List Top 100 Employers 2018." https://www.stonewall. org.uk/full-list-top-100-employers-2018.
The National Assembly for Wales came first as LGBT-friendly, and Fujitsu ranked last. In between, we find the Royal Navy and Marines (no. 32), MI6 (no. 49), and the British Army (no. 84).

"Anthropolesbos." DDT21. https://ddt21.noblogs.org/?page_id=1850.

Weeks, Jeffrey. "Questions of Identity." In Pat Caplan, ed. *The Cultural Construction of Sexuality.* London: Routledge, 1987.

Chapter 13: Meanwhile, in The Rest of the World…

AIDS Analysis Asia. Cited in Pierre Tremblay and Richard Ramsay, *The Changing Social Construction of Male Homosexuality…, Male Homosexuality: From Common to a Rarity,* 2000–2004. https://people. ucalgary.ca/~ramsay/suicide-homosexuality/index.htm.

Brodie, Fawn. *The Devil Rides: A Life of Sir Richard Burton.* New York: Penguin, 1971.

Burton, Richard, trans. "Terminal Essay." In *Arabians Nights,* vol. 10, 63–65. London: Burton Club, 1886. https://ia802700.us.archive.org/27/ items/plainliteraltran10burtuoft/plainliteraltran10burtuoft.pdf. *Burton discusses what he means by "Sodatic Zone."*

Chiang, Howard H. "Post-Colonial Historiography, Queer Historiography." http://interalia.org.pl/index_pdf.php?lang=en&klucz=&produkt= 1199709173-369.

Friese, Kal. "Porn Star in U.S., Starlet in Bollywood." *International New York Times,* May 9–10, 2015.

Genç, Kaya. "Sex Changes in Turkey." *New York Review of Books,* June 28, 2018. https://www.nybooks.com/articles/2018/06/28/sex-changes-in-turkey.

Moodie, T. Dunbar. "Migrancy and Male Sexuality in the South African Gold Mines." In Martin Duberman and Martha Vicinus. *Hidden from History: Reclaiming the Gay and Lesbian Past.* New York: Meridian, 1990.

Nanda, Serena. "Hijras: An Alternative Sex and Gender Role in India." In Gilbert Herdt, ed. *Third Sex, Third Gender.* Brooklyn, NY: Zone Books, 2020.

Chapter 14: New Moral (Dis)Order

Califia, Pat [now Patrick]. *Public Sex: The Culture of Radical Sex.* Hoboken, NJ: Cleis Press, 1994.

Chiang, Howard H. "Post-Colonial Historiography, Queer Historiography." http://interalia.org.pl/index_pdf.php?lang=en&klucz=&prod ukt=1199709173-369.

Dauvé, Gilles. "On the 'Woman Question'" (2016). https://troploin.fr/node/88.
Discusses the subjugation of women.

Dauvé, Gilles. *White Riot, 1922: Race & Class in 20th Century South Africa* (2018). https://theanarchistlibrary.org/library/gilles-dauve-white-riot-1922.
Addresses the division between proletarians, with special reference to race.

D'Emilio, John. "Capitalism and Gay Identity." In Henry Abelove, Michèle Aina Barale, and David M. Halperin, eds. *The Lesbian and Gay Studies Reader.* New York: Routledge, 1993.

Duberman, Martin, and Martha Vicinus. *Hidden from History: Reclaiming the Gay and Lesbian Past.* New York: Meridian, 1990.

Gabriel, Mary. *Love and Capital: Karl and Jenny Marx and the Birth of a Revolution.* New York: Bay Back Books, 2012.

Harrison, A.S.A. *The Silent Wife.* London: Penguin, 2013.

Kapp, Yvonne. *Eleanor Marx: A Biography.* London: Verso, 2018.

Katz, Jonathan. *The Invention of Heterosexuality.* Chicago: University of Chicago Press, 2007 [1995].

Kendrick, Walter. *The Secret Museum: Pornography in Modern Culture.* Berkeley, CA: University of California Press, 1997.

Laqueur, Thomas. *Making Sex: Body and Gender from the Greeks to Freud.* Cambridge, MA: Harvard University Press, 1990. https://tinyurl.com/4y27stm9.
Laqueur stressed the shift in the eighteenth century from the "one-body" to the "two-body" model: the female form came to be conceived as the opposite of the male rather than as a variation on it.

Miller, Neil. *Out of the Past: Gay and Lesbian History from 1869 to the Present.* New York: Vintage Books, 1995.

Mitchell, Eve. *I Am a Woman and a Human: A Marxist Critique of Intersectionality Theory.* libcom.org. September 12, 2013. https://tinyurl.com/2p89vf7w.

Sono, Sion, dir. *Love Exposure.* Tokyo: Omega Project, 2009.

Tombs, Robert. *The English and Their History.* London: Penguin, 2014, chapter 10.

Tremblay, Pierre, and Richard Ramsay. *The Changing Social Construction of Male Homosexuality…, Male Homosexuality: From Common to a Rarity,* 2000–2004. https://people.ucalgary.ca/~ramsay/suicide-homosexuality/index.htmhttps://people.ucalgary.ca/~ramsay/suicide-homosexuality/index.htmhttps://people.ucalgary.ca/~ramsay/suicide-homosexuality/index.htm.
By the 1920s, many American psychologists viewed child or teenage homosexual experience as a transitory and quite normal phase. Tremblay and Ramsay address this: "In 1960, I was 10-years-old and

growing up in a working class community where homosexual activity between young male friends was common, not the exception. Its predominant manifestation was 'sex with equality,' that included mutual masturbation and oral sex, but not anal sex.... The latter was not even thought about, except for eventually learning that passive anal sex was an activity engaged in by apparently degraded males who thought themselves to be like women, or were labeled as such because they were accepting the status of being anally penetrated. Effeminate males with apparent or perceived feminine manners or characteristics did not exist in our community."

Welzer-Lang, Daniel. *Les nouvelles hétérosexualités*. Toulouse, FR: Erès, 2018.

"What's in an Acronym? Parsing the LGBTQQIP2SAA Community." Social Justice for All. https://tinyurl.com/y4mzzh8x.

White, Edmund. "I Do, I Do." *New York Review of Books*, August 14, 2014. http://www.nybooks.com/articles/2014/08/14/i-do-i-do.
For a short excerpt, see https://www.pbs.org/wgbh/pages/frontline/shows/assault/context/katzhistory.html.

Troubled and uncertain situations inevitably give birth to a "reactionary" backlash. In the first decades of the twentieth century, pro-masculinity, anti-feminist moods and groups appeared, especially in Germany, as well as in the Italian Futurist movement led by Filippo Tommaso Marinetti (on Germany, see note at the end of the bibliography for chapter 5). Similarly, a male movement along the lines of "it's great to be straight" has emerged in opposition to what it regards as its LGBT "oppressors." Copying LGBT methods, it has its "Straight Pride Day," its "awareness month," and even its own colors, a black and white flag, with a marked preference for black. ("Show your support by wearing something black. Even a black ribbon will do.") It also has an extreme racist wing, the "straight white man," e.g., the Proud Boys.

Postlude: Polysex

Baudelaire, Charles. "Lesbos." https://lyricstranslate.com/en/lesbos-lesbos.html.
"Lesbos" was one of six poems from Flowers of Evil *censored by court order in 1857, on the grounds that they were immoral and obscene, as well as morbid, Satanist, etc. These poems were published in 1866, but the judgment was only officially lifted in 1949.*

Blanc, Dominique, *A World without Money: Communism—Les Amis de 4 Millions de Jeunes Travailleurs, 1975–1976*. https://tinyurl.com/4rsy55me.

Chamberland, Line. *Mémoires lesbiennes, Le Lesbianisme à Montréal entre 1950 et 1972*. Montréal: Éditions du remue-ménage, 1996.

Dauvé, Gilles. *Moral Disorder and Sexual Identity* (2003). https://troploin.fr/node/36.

Includes an extract from Browning, Frank. A Queer Geography: Journeys toward a Sexual Self, rev. ed. Farrar, Straus & Giroux, 1998 [1996].

"For a World without a Moral Order," *La Banquise* no. 1, (1983; updated regarding Charles Fourier's *New Amorous World*, 2014). https://troploin.fr/node/77.

Shainberg, Steven, dir. *Secretary*. New York: TwoPoundBag Productions, 2002.

About the Author

Born in 1947, Gilles Dauvé has worked as a translator and school teacher. He is the author of essays and books translated into many languages on the Russian, German, and Spanish Revolutions, as well as the Situationist International, democracy, fascism, war, morals, crisis, and class, some under the pseudonym Jean Barrot. He also had two novels published in French in 1992 and 1998. In 2014, the PM Press Revolutionary Pocketbooks series published an expanded edition of his collection of essays *Eclipse and Re-Emergence of the Communist Movement*. In 2015, he wrote "An A to Z of Communisation" in *Everything Must Go! The Abolition of Value*, a book co-authored with Bruno Astarian (Little Black Cart Books).

In 2019, the PM Press Revolutionary Pocketbooks published his *From Crisis to Communisation*. A number of both his earlier and more recent texts can be found on the www.troploin.fr website.

ABOUT PM PRESS

PM Press is an independent, radical publisher of books and media to educate, entertain, and inspire. Founded in 2007 by a small group of people with decades of publishing, media, and organizing experience, PM Press amplifies the voices of radical authors, artists, and activists. Our aim is to deliver bold political ideas and vital stories to all walks of life and arm the dreamers to demand the impossible. We have sold millions of copies of our books, most often one at a time, face to face. We're old enough to know what we're doing and young enough to know what's at stake. Join us to create a better world.

PM Press
PO Box 23912
Oakland, CA 94623
www.pmpress.org

PM Press in Europe
europe@pmpress.org
www.pmpress.org.uk

FRIENDS OF PM PRESS

These are indisputably momentous times—the financial system is melting down globally and the Empire is stumbling. Now more than ever there is a vital need for radical ideas.

In the many years since its founding—and on a mere shoestring—PM Press has risen to the formidable challenge of publishing and distributing knowledge and entertainment for the struggles ahead. With hundreds of releases to date, we have published an impressive and stimulating array of literature, art, music, politics, and culture. Using every available medium, we've succeeded in connecting those hungry for ideas and information to those putting them into practice.

Friends of PM allows you to directly help impact, amplify, and revitalize the discourse and actions of radical writers, filmmakers, and artists. It provides us with a stable foundation from which we can build upon our early successes and provides a much-needed subsidy for the materials that can't necessarily pay their own way. You can help make that happen—and receive every new title automatically delivered to your door once a month—by joining as a Friend of PM Press. And, we'll throw in a free T-shirt when you sign up.

Here are your options:

- **$30 a month** Get all books and pamphlets plus 50% discount on all webstore purchases

- **$40 a month** Get all PM Press releases (including CDs and DVDs) plus 50% discount on all webstore purchases

- **$100 a month** Superstar—Everything plus PM merchandise, free downloads, and 50% discount on all webstore purchases

For those who can't afford $30 or more a month, we have **Sustainer Rates** at $15, $10 and $5. Sustainers get a free PM Press T-shirt and a 50% discount on all purchases from our website.

Your Visa or Mastercard will be billed once a month, until you tell us to stop. Or until our efforts succeed in bringing the revolution around. Or the financial meltdown of Capital makes plastic redundant. Whichever comes first.

Eclipse and Re-emergence of the Communist Movement

Gilles Dauvé and François Martin

ISBN: 978-1-62963-043-4
$14.95   168 pages

In the years following 1968, a number of people involved in the most radical aspects of the French general strike felt the need to reflect on their experiences and to relate them to past revolutionary endeavors. This meant studying previous attempts and theories, namely those of the post-1917 German-Dutch and Italian Communist Left. The original essays included here were first written between 1969 and 1972 and circulated amongst left communist and worker circles.

But France was not the only country where radicals sought to contextualize their political environment and analyze their own radical pasts. Over the years these three essays have been published separately in various languages and printed as books in both the United States and the UK with few changes. This third English edition is updated to take into account the contemporary political situation; half of the present volume is new material.

The book argues that doing away with wage-labor, class, the State, and private property is necessary, possible, and can only be achieved by a historical break, one that would certainly differ from October 1917 . . . yet it would not be a peaceful, gradual, piecemeal evolution either. Like their historical predecessors—Marx, Rosa Luxemburg, Anton Pannekoek, Amadeo Bordiga, Durruti, and Debord—the authors maintain a belief in revolution.

"Gilles Dauvé is well-known in certain circles for his radical ideas about the functioning of modern capitalist society. The author has had a significant influence on both libertarian communists and anarchists."
—Iš rankų į rankas press (Lithuania)

From Crisis to Communisation

Gilles Dauvé

ISBN: 978-1-62963-099-1
$16.95   192 pages

"Communisation" means something quite straightforward: a revolution that starts to change social relations immediately. It would extend over years, decades probably, but from Day One it would begin to do away with wage-labour, profit, productivity, private property, classes, States, masculine domination, etc. There would be no "transition period" in the Marxist sense, no period when the "associated producers" continue furthering economic growth to create the industrial foundations of a new world. Communisation means a creative insurrection that would bring about communism, not its preconditions.

Thus stated, it sounds simple enough. The questions are what, how, and by whom. That is what this book is about.

Communisation is not the be-all and end-all that solves everything and proves wrong all past critical theory. The concept was born out of a specific period, and we can fully understand it by going back to how people personally and collectively experienced the crises of the 1960s and '70s. The notion is now developing in the maelstrom of a new crisis, deeper than the Depression of the 1930s, among other reasons because of its ecological dimension, a crisis that has the scope and magnitude of a crisis of civilisation.

This is not a book that glorifies existing struggles as if their present accumulation was enough to result in revolution. Radical theory is meaningful if it addresses this question: how can proletarian resistance to exploitation and dispossession achieve more than aggravate the crisis? How can it reshape the world?

"Gilles Dauvé is well-known in certain circles for his radical ideas about the functioning of modern capitalist society. The author has had a significant influence on both libertarian communists and anarchists."
—Iš rankų į rankas press (Lithuania)

Queercore: How to Punk a Revolution: An Oral History

Edited by Liam Warfield, Walter Crasshole, and Yony Leyser with an Introduction by Anna Joy Springer and Lynn Breedlove

ISBN: 978-1-62963-796-9
$18.00   208 pages

Queercore: How to Punk a Revolution: An Oral History is the very first comprehensive overview of a movement that defied both the music underground and the LGBT mainstream community.

Through exclusive interviews with protagonists like Bruce LaBruce, G.B. Jones, Jayne County, Kathleen Hanna of Bikini Kill and Le Tigre, film director and author John Waters, Lynn Breedlove of Tribe 8, Jon Ginoli of Pansy Division, and many more, alongside a treasure trove of never-before-seen photographs and reprinted zines from the time, *Queercore* traces the history of a scene originally "fabricated" in the bedrooms and coffee shops of Toronto and San Francisco by a few young, queer punks to its emergence as a relevant and real revolution. *Queercore* is a down-to-details firsthand account of the movement explored by the people that lived it—from punk's early queer elements, to the moment that Toronto kids decided they needed to create a scene that didn't exist, to Pansy Division's infiltration of the mainstream, and the emergence of riot grrrl—as well as the clothes, zines, art, film, and music that made this movement an exciting middle finger to complacent gay and straight society. *Queercore* will stand as both a testament to radically gay politics and culture and an important reference for those who wish to better understand this explosive movement.

"Finally, a book that centers on the wild, innovative, and fearless contributions queers made to punk rock, creating a punker-than-punk subculture beneath the subculture, Queercore. *Gossipy and inspiring, a historical document and a call to arms during a time when the entire planet could use a dose of queer, creative rage."*
—Michelle Tea, author of *Valencia*

Y'all Means All: The Emerging Voices Queering Appalachia

Edited by Z. Zane McNeill

ISBN: 978-1-62963-914-7
$20.00   200 pages

Y'all Means All is a celebration of the weird and wonderful aspects of a troubled region in all of their manifest glory! This collection is a thought-provoking hoot and a holler of "we're queer and we're here to stay, cause we're every bit a piece of the landscape as the rocks and the trees" echoing through the hills of Appalachia and into the boardrooms of every media outlet and opportunistic author seeking to define Appalachia from the outside for their own political agendas. Multidisciplinary and multi-genre, *Y'all* necessarily incorporates elements of critical theory, such as critical race theory and queer theory, while dealing with a multitude of methodologies, from quantitative analysis, to oral history and autoethnography.

This collection eschews the contemporary trend of "reactive" or "responsive" writing in the genre of Appalachian studies, and alternatively, provides examples of how modern Appalachians are defining themselves on their own terms. As such, it also serves as a toolkit for other Appalachian readers to follow suit, and similarly challenge the labels, stereotypes and definitions often thrust upon them. While providing blunt commentary on the region's past and present, the book's soul is sustained by the resilience, ingenuity, and spirit exhibited by the authors; values which have historically characterized the Appalachian region and are continuing to define its culture to the present.

This book demonstrates above all else that Appalachia and its people are filled with a vitality and passion for their region which will slowly but surely effect long-lasting and positive changes in the region. If historically Appalachia has been treated as a "mirror" of the country, this book breaks that trend by allowing modern Appalachians to examine their own reflections and to share their insights in an honest, unfiltered manner with the world.

Facebooking the Anthropocene in Raja Ampat: Technics and Civilization in the 21st Century

Bob Ostertag

ISBN: 978-1-62963-830-0
$17.00   192 pages

The three essays of *Facebooking the Anthropocene in Raja Ampat* paint a deeply intimate portrait of the cataclysmic shifts between humans, technology, and the so-called natural world. Amid the breakneck pace of both technological advance and environmental collapse, Bob Ostertag explores how we are changing as fast as the world around us—from how we make music, to how we have sex, to what we do to survive, and who we imagine ourselves to be. And though the environmental crisis terrifies and technology overwhelms, Ostertag finds enough creativity, compassion, and humor in our evolving behavior to keep us laughing and inspired as the world we are building overtakes the world we found.

A true polymath who covered the wars in Central America during the 1980s, recorded dozens of music projects, and published books on startlingly eclectic subjects, Ostertag fuses his travels as a touring musician with his journalist's eye for detail and the long view of a historian. Wander both the physical and the intellectual world with him. Watch Buddhist monks take selfies while meditating and DJs who make millions of dollars pretend to turn knobs in front of crowds of thousands. Shiver with families huddling through the stinging Detroit winter without heat or electricity. Meet Spice Islanders who have never seen flushing toilets yet have gay hookup apps on their phones.

Our best writers have struggled with how to address the catastrophes of our time without looking away. Ostertag succeeds where others have failed, with the moral acuity of Susan Sontag, the technological savvy of Lewis Mumford, and the biting humor of Jonathan Swift.

"With deep intelligence and an acute and off-center sensibility, Robert Ostertag gives us a riveting and highly personalized view of globalization, from the soaring skyscapes of Shanghai to the darkened alleys of Yogyakarta."
—Frances Fox Piven, coauthor of *Regulating the Poor* and *Poor People's Movements*

Crisis and Care: Queer Activist Responses to a Global Pandemic

Adrian Shanker
with a Foreword by Rea Carey

ISBN: 978-1-62963-935-2
$15.95   128 pages

Crisis and Care reveals what is possible when activists mobilize for the radical changes our society needs. In a time of great uncertainty, fear, and isolation, Queer activists organized for health equity, prison abolition, racial justice, and more. Nobody who lived through the COVID-19 pandemic will soon forget the challenges, sacrifices, and incredible loss felt during such an uncertain time in history. *Crisis and Care* anthologizes not what happened during COVID-19, or why it happened, but rather how Queer activists responded in real time. It considers the necessity to memorialize resiliency as well as loss, hope as well as pain, to remember the strides forward as well as the steps back. Activist contributors Zephyr Williams, Mark Travis Rivera, Jamie Gliksburg, Denise Spivak, Emmett Patterson, Omar Gonzales-Pagan, Kenyon Farrow, and more provide a radical lens through which future activists can consider effective strategies to make change, even or perhaps especially, during periods of crisis.

"Adrian Shanker has emerged in recent years as an urgent and prescient voice on matters concerning queer health. Crisis and Care: Queer Activist Responses to a Global Pandemic *is timely, important and shares a message we ignore at our own peril. The response to COVID-19 from LGBTQ communities is informed by our own experience with a deadly pandemic made vastly worse by poor presidential leadership. Our lived experience over the past 40 years has valuable lessons for how we should be addressing today's viral threats."*
—Sean Strub, author of *Body Counts: A Memoir of Politics, Sex, AIDS, and Survival*

"How did we respond? That is the central question in Crisis and Care. *Lots of books will look at COVID-19, but this book looks at how LGBTQ activists responded to one of the most challenging moments of our lives."*
—Igor Volsky, author of *Guns Down: How to Defeat the NRA and Build a Safer Future with Fewer Guns*